Finding My Voice

Finding My Voice

EMERALD GARNER

with ETAN THOMAS and MONET DUNHAM

Afterword by ILYASAH SHABAZZ

Haymarket Books
Chicago, Illinois

Published in 2022 by
Haymarket Books
P.O. Box 180165
Chicago, IL 60618
773-583-7884
www.haymarketbooks.org
info@haymarketbooks.org

ISBN: 978-1-64259-831-5

Distributed to the trade in the US through Consortium Book Sales and Distribution (www.cbsd.com) and internationally through Ingram Publisher Services International (www.ingramcontent.com).

This book was published with the generous support of Lannan Foundation and Wallace Action Fund.

Special discounts are available for bulk purchases by organizations and institutions. Please email info@haymarketbooks.org for more information.

Cover photograph by Javon Acree, IMU Media.
Cover design by Rachel Cohen.

Printed in Canada by union labor.

Library of Congress Cataloging-in-Publication data is available.

10 9 8 7 6 5 4 3 2 1

CONTENTS

CHAPTER 1

They Killed My Father

July 17, 2014, started out as a normal day. It was the middle of the summer, and the heat was insufferable—it was hot, unbearably hot! I had no idea that my life was about to change forever. I never imagined what was in store. I was home with my friend Breanna and our kids, Kaylee and Kory. We had just eaten breakfast and were about to spend the day relaxing in the house. It was my day off, and I was looking forward to relaxing. I was working at Payless as a key person (an assistant manager). I had been on the job for about two months. I was feeling pretty good about myself. I was feeling accomplished. I had worked very hard to advance myself. I was happy about being independent. I had my own apartment. I was feeling my adulthood.

My phone rang. It was a call from my mother, and she was frantic. She said, "Your father was rushed to the hospital from Bay Street, and they said he's not breathing." I said, "He's not breathing, or did he have an asthma attack?" She said she didn't know and would call me back.

I told my friend to watch the kids and that I would be right back. I went out to the store and ended up calling another friend of mine, Kiara, who didn't live far from me. I told her what was going on, and she said, "Make the call three-way and call your mother again," so I did. When I called, my mother didn't answer. Kiara said, "I think you should head to Staten Island ASAP!" I remember feeling so nervous and uneasy, like I was ready to jump out of my skin. I tried to call all my siblings then I headed back upstairs. No one answered the phone.

When I got back up to my house, I tried to call again. My mom picked up and said she was heading to the hospital and would call me back. I was getting pissed off because I wanted answers, and I wanted them now! I looked at my friend Breanna and said, "I don't know what to do." She said, "I don't know why you still sitting in my face! If that was my father, I would have been left." I was feeling crazy and told her, "I don't want to overreact, but OK I'm about to head out now." I called my mother and told her I was on my way. Breanna agreed to watch Kaylee.

I hopped on the train and headed to Staten Island and began praying so hard. The entire time I prayed harder than I have ever prayed before. I said, "God, please don't let my father be gone by the time I get there, please don't let this happen. I know me and my father don't really see eye to eye on many things, but I don't want him to die. Please let him be OK so I can tell him how much I love him and how sorry I am for being a rebellious teen and how I am sorry for the yelling, the cursing, the fighting, and all the stress I caused growing up, and if you would just keep him safe I promise to do better in my life and be a better daughter and a better sibling and an overall better person if you would just let my daddy live."

I remember thinking there were so many things I didn't understand as a child. I was just beginning to understand them as an adult. My father and I were working through so many unresolved issues, and I couldn't believe it could just be over like this! "No way God will do this to me," I thought. Not now, not *ever*! We were a work in progress, and nobody understood me or our relationship better than my father.

I was so spaced out heading to Staten Island that I thought people were looking at me like I was crazy. I had to take the 6 train to the 5 train and then take a ferry and then get on the bus. I didn't know what bus I needed to take from the ferry so I called my mother and said, "I'm on the Staten Island side. What bus should I take to the hospital?" When she answered, her voice was shaky and she said, "Come home, Emerald. . . He's gone. . . He died at the hospital. . . There was nothing else they could do." I remember asking what she meant, since I didn't believe he could be gone.

She said that I should just come to the house. I got on the bus heading to my mother's house. I was on the bus standing because the bus was crowded. I remember stepping off the bus and immediately feeling a sense of uneasiness, like I was going to faint. I began to slowly and cautiously walk up the street, so I didn't lose my balance and pass out, and I could see my mother and a few other people in front of the building. I walked up and just broke down crying. I couldn't hold back my emotions any longer. I began to ask questions, and I was told that when she got to the hospital doors they said they "were working on him for an hour or so." My mom said she kept getting short answers from the police, and she was crying hysterically while attempting to explain what happened at the hospital. She ended up telling me that my father was choked to death by the police, there was a video, and we were waiting for more information. I was distraught. I went into the house to check on my little brother Emery. He was on the couch looking really odd and out of it. I asked him the most stupid and dumb question I could have possibly asked him, and to this day I regret ever saying it, but I asked, "Are you all right?" He immediately broke down crying, and I hugged him tight and held him close. I could feel his heart beating. I wished I could take the pain away from him. I wish I could have taken it away from myself. I felt so helpless. Emotions of anger, sadness, and literal pain were running through my body all at the same time.

I went back outside and asked my mother where my father's stuff was. She said, "They gave me his clothes and shoes, they're in the house." I asked her, "Where's the car?" She said it was "still on Bay Street by the check cashing place." I told her I would go get it, so me and the woman that lived upstairs from my mother, Fatima, went to go get it. I also wanted to see what was going on at the scene. We took the bus over to Bay Street and walked around by the Dominos to see what was happening. I saw a group of people and a lot of cops and cop cars and police tape. I walked over to the car, and I saw a few people watching me, police included. I sat in the car for a minute before I took off. I was sitting there thinking about crashing the car through the group of police standing there because I knew they had something to do with the killing of my father. I was so pissed off, I was ready to do and say some crazy stuff. I ended up driving the car back to Jersey Street, where my mother lived, and just giving her the stuff that was in the car—the cigarettes and the money that my father left in the car. We were outside talking for a bit. I don't exactly remember what was said, but I know they were talking about the situation and the different sides of the story that everyone was putting together.

After what felt like hours of sitting in the car, I went back to the building and by that time everyone was gathered at my mother's house. My father's stepfather, Ben, came over and said he was taking my father's car to park it in the garage. I offered to take the car back to Manhattan and keep it so I could get back to Staten Island the next day. My mother told me that Ben was going to take the car, and that didn't sit well with me at all. I guess it was because no one was listening to me and thought they knew what was best. I wanted to keep the car a little longer because it was the last thing left of his memory, and I wanted it—not to keep forever, but to have for the time being and so that I would have a definite way of getting back to Staten Island. I ended up giving in because it was clearly a battle I wasn't going to win. I didn't say I was broke and needed the ride, because no one would care, they just wanted to do what they wanted to do and that was it. Truth be told, I was actually broke and had about ten dollars when the day started, and I had used five to get to Staten Island. I didn't say anything though and no one asked either. A man from the *Daily News* called my mother and said there was a video of my father's murder. The guy who filmed it was in a hotel for safety reasons, and the reporter was coming to my mother's house to ask some questions. From that moment on I knew things were going to get crazy, and I was right.

CHAPTER 2

Media Exploitation

After my father was murdered, I started attending the National Action Network Youth Huddle on Mondays, and that's really where I started to learn about the history of civil rights and the power of protesting. So one day in particular during one of the meetings, it was suggested that we consider doing a mass action because two police officers were killed by a man who was battling mental issues, but the media were pushing the narrative that he had done this as a retaliation for my father being killed by the police—not that this was a direct result of someone having a mental health issue, which, coincidentally, they have no problems saying whenever there is a mass shooting. They wanted to make the story that this man killed these police officers in the name of Eric Garner as payback to the NYPD.

I was hesitant at first because I didn't want my presence to be turned into something else or weaponized to start a riot, which is what I saw the media attempting to do with their headlines and stories. I didn't want to take any attention away from the police officers' families. I didn't want to offend anyone. So I was extremely skeptical, but what changed my mind was when I started to read about the young children who were left behind and were now fatherless like I was. If it weren't for that, I probably would've stayed out of it, but I thought about those young children and the pain and agony they must've been going through and how I wouldn't wish that on anyone. And they were young. Me and my siblings were all relatively grown. Emery was the youngest, but he was well into his teens. These kids were single-digit young, and it hurt my heart that they would be going through life dealing with this trauma.

I decided to extend my personal condolences to them and the families. I wanted to tell them not to let this break them down. I wanted to remind them of how it's already broken us down. I went into action. My plan was to lay the wreath, join in the prayer. I prepared a statement just in case but hoped to keep a low profile. The media and the cameras wouldn't allow that to happen though. As soon as I was spotted, they literally ambushed me. There was a picture in the paper and you could see me in the middle of a sea of cameras and media looking overwhelmed. I didn't expect that type of reaction at all. And the questions they began to throw at me were just vicious. They were obviously trying to create a headline and a narrative.

They started with, "Is this in retaliation for Eric Garner?" "Do you feel responsible for these police officers being murdered?" "Do you hate all police?" I was really shocked that they would ask me some of those questions. It was just heartless and cruel, but that was my introduction to how the media attempts to manipulate a situation for headlines and clicks.

But to add to that, I also had so many people from the community reaching out to me personally to convey their disapproval of me for showing any sympathy whatsoever for the police who were killed. They were actually mad at me! Saying things like, "How could you do that?" "Your father is rolling over in his grave right now." "How could you stand with the people who killed your father?"

And again I was amazed at how callous and cruel people can be, but now it's my people, people of color, who are being cruel. People who look like me, who I personally know and some who I don't know, and again I was shocked. How do they feel qualified to tell me what they would do if they were in my position? The fact is, they aren't. It's my father who was murdered, who the media shows being killed over and over again like trauma porn that people can't get enough of. Who are they to tell me how I should cope with this? Unless they have literally had the police murder their father, they have no idea how I feel.

And furthermore, these weren't the same policemen who killed my father. The cop who murdered my father, Eric Garner, is named Daniel Pantaleo. These are cops who were minding their business, doing their jobs, patrolling whatever area they were assigned to patrol, and someone murdered them. Why would I not feel bad for their families and loved ones? They didn't have anything to do with my father being killed. I want to show these kids some support and some love the same way I wanted to receive love and support after my father was killed, and it hurt that so many people, again, people who look like me, started really criticizing and bashing me from every angle. I actually got hate mail, which is absolutely crazy. I am trying to support some kids who had their provider, their protector, their father, taken from them, and people can't understand why I would feel moved to support them? But that's where I learned that a lot of people will only support you on their terms.

CHAPTER 3

Mental Health

When I was a teenager, I spent some time in the foster care system. We were removed from my mother because it was deemed at the time that she was unfit to care for us. I was fifteen and my sister Erica was sixteen and a half, and they took me and my brothers but left my sister. That made me think my mother wanted my sister more than she wanted me, that she didn't love me as much as she loved her, that she didn't want to deal with me and that's why I was in foster care. That's how my young teenage mind interpreted the situation. On top of that, I wasn't in the same foster home as my brothers, which caused more internal struggles for me. The reality is that my brothers were sent to another home because younger kids are easier to place in foster homes, and Children's Services allowed Erica to stay with my mom because she was sixteen and a half. At fifteen, I was too young to stay home. But again, that's not how my teenage mind interpreted the situation. I took it as rejection. So I was internally damaged from that.

I was angry with my father for a long time because I concluded that I must not have been special enough or important enough to him since he allowed me to be taken into foster care, and it wasn't until I was older that I was able to see that it was out of his hands, because once the system takes over they decide which child goes where, how long they stay there, and they don't care about keeping a family together. So it took me years of therapy to be able to deal with that. Years of going through different therapists who couldn't relate to me and couldn't help me deal with what I was dealing with and the internal struggles I was having. In foster care, they usually assign a therapist to the children, especially if they see the slightest sign of problems, or issues, or acting out. But many times, it's people who don't really know what they're doing. Almost like they're getting their practice before they become real therapists. Or like court-appointed attorneys who don't know all of the particulars about the case and are given the file minutes before they have to go into court.

There were times I was so happy as a child. Christmas was great! We got lots of gifts, and we always had fun. We went to Six Flags amusement park every year with Pfizer, because that's where Gramma worked. We took vacations and made trips to Baltimore. We used to go to a big family picnic with the Braxton side of the family. We always did stuff for Easter, mainly go to the circus, which was our favorite part of Easter. That all stopped when we were removed from our parents.

I remember one lady, who was a nice lady who happened to be Asian American, and she was assigned to me for a period of time. Now, this lady couldn't relate to me. I was a young Black girl from the projects who felt rejected by her family and thrown into the foster care system to literally fight for her life, and this lady was asking me to draw some pictures about happy thoughts? I was looking at her like, "Are you serious? Happy thoughts? Happy places to take my mind to? OK, maybe you didn't hear what I said I was dealing with?" That's why I always say that the wrong kind of therapy can be more harmful than no therapy at all. They weren't properly dealing with my mental health. I tell this story to set the groundwork for how I would see how important mental health is after I lost my father. In my opinion, this is something this society as a whole doesn't take seriously enough. Fortunately, I was eventually placed with a therapist named Robin. She was young and she was Black. I liked that she lived on her own. She was easier to relate to. I really enjoyed talking to her.

Fast forward to the aftermath of my father's murder. I always say, "If mental health had been a priority, a lot of the issues I had with my family after my father was taken from us wouldn't have happened." I can't stress enough how important mental health is after a tragedy like this, what it does to the family structure. It destroyed all of us, and we were forced to attempt to build back the pieces of our broken structure on our own.

Let me start with myself. It would have been helpful for me to have someone to talk to about all the emotions and tragedy I was feeling. I had nobody to talk to. Who was going to make this make sense for me? Now, historically, in our community, therapy is kind of taboo. It's not something that's discussed or embraced. I think we have been forced to endure so much for so long, going back to slavery, and we were always taught to suck it up and keep pushing along. We never had the luxury of talking about our trauma and our feelings, we always had to be in survival mode, because only the strong survived. If we would've been focused on how horrible our situation really was, we would've crumbled. So the mentality got passed down from generation to generation that we don't talk about our problems, our issues, our feelings, we just tuck them deep down somewhere in the abyss of our emotions and keep going.

But I needed therapy, counseling, mental health nurturing, and everything else, and so did my entire family.

I have had therapy in the past that didn't work. When you go through the foster care system like I did, one of the things that happens is you are assigned a therapist, but it was the wrong kind of therapist for me. I didn't relate to her, and she didn't relate to me. It actually made things worse to be honest because I began to get frustrated at this lady who couldn't understand where I was coming from, couldn't understand my pain, my suffering, and was giving me these cookie-cutter solutions that weren't right for me. I had abandonment issues and used to lay awake at night hoping someone would come save me. When that didn't happen, I had to learn how to save myself.

As I am older looking back on it, I can see now that I just didn't have a good setup, but this did give me a negative feeling toward therapy as a whole. The fact is, the wrong kind of therapy can actually be more detrimental than no therapy at all. I needed therapy back then, and I needed it right away. I actually had a relapse of my abandonment issues after my father was taken away from me. The amount of emotions I was personally feeling was all over the place, and I needed help dealing with it.

So let me be clear, what me and my entire family needed was the right kind of therapy. And for me, I was forced to deal alone with the trauma, and the anxiety, and the roaming thoughts and emotions after my father was murdered, I recognize that it would have been very helpful if someone had come in as a mental health professional, and not only for myself but also for my mother, my sister, my brothers, and everyone else in my family. We didn't have bereavement counseling. In fact, I've never in my life been to a bereavement counseling session. I didn't even know that bereavement counseling existed, and now that I am learning about it, I wish that would've been available to me and my family.

So as a result, the issues that we had before my father was killed remained after his murder and were magnified times a thousand. With bereavement counseling, we would've been able to deal with the issues of the past, deal with the issues of the present, and have a plan for the future. But there were no steps, no nothing, it was, "Just don't worry about it," "Down the line everything will be fine," and "Once you get the settlement, everything will be OK." And that couldn't be farther from the truth. There was no togetherness, no accountability for the world mishandling us.

So here's how it went. My father is murdered then boom we're thrown in front of the camera, boom we're speaking at the National Action Network (NAN), and the next month we're all over the world because we're doing a march someplace else with NAN. Then the next month Mike Brown is killed, and the next month Sandra Bland is killed. And while you haven't even fully grieved, you're now linked to other cases, and you only have the bond that your loved one was also murdered by the police. And you have to navigate being retraumatized over and over again while you still haven't received justice for your father being murdered, and the video is being played over and over and over again, and the cop who committed the murder and all of the cops who stood around and watched and didn't intervene or say, "OK that's enough," or, "He's said he can't breathe eleven times," or, "He's down, stop choking him," are just living their lives, back with their families, back to work like nothing happened. And through all of this, there was nobody pulling us to the side saying, "Hey, I've dealt with families who have experienced trauma, and you can use these methods to cope," or, "You need to talk to this person who will help guide you through this process." There was nothing. And we all grieve differently, every one of us because we are different people and need different things and that's why, going back to what I said earlier, the right kind of therapy and counseling is needed. But also, all that costs money. None of that is free. The surviving family members of a victim of police brutality should all automatically get all of the counseling and therapy they need free of charge for as long as they need it. That should be automatic.

I personally don't like to deal with things head-on, so I become a hermit crab. You don't hear from me for a while, you may see a few social media posts here and there, but you won't see me calling and texting a lot because I am in healing mode for myself and feel I have to shut out everyone else in the world. With the right guidance, I would have learned that, although I may need that, I should warn the people close to me before I go quiet. Or I should communicate the best way to be there for me and the way not to attempt to be there for me because sometimes people have to be taught how to support you and can't read your mind or your emotions. But I didn't have anyone guiding me through that, and relationships were damaged as a result.

Erica was different. She wanted to let the world know exactly how she felt. She wanted to be open with her emotions. She wanted to wear her heart on her sleeve, and for everyone to be fully aware of what she was going through, struggling with, and dealing with. She wanted to rally the troops and storm the castle, so to speak. She wanted to scream from the mountaintops with a megaphone.

My brother Eric wanted to busy himself with partying to take his mind off everything. Almost as if he didn't want to think about everything going on, so he tried to replace it with people and music and partying. But in his quiet moments, he was tormented about it and had difficulty speaking about it in private or in public.

My other brother Emery, the youngest, just digressed completely. He went into babyism. He couldn't deal with it at all without breaking down. And that was the same for all of us. We just presented it differently. He needed someone to help push him along because the world doesn't stop just because you have stopped. The world keeps going. And he needed someone to guide him through managing all of that.

Everyone started to grieve differently, and nobody was given the proper tools that should have been applied to each way of grieving. So we were all left to figure it out for ourselves, and we shouldn't have had to do that. We didn't choose for my father to be murdered, but we were left to pick up the pieces after, and that just wasn't fair.

I was speaking to Ms. Lora Dene King, who is the daughter of Rodney King, and she was explaining to me how detrimental it was for her father that he never received counseling after he was beaten by the police. He had PTSD and turned to self-medicating later because he had no help. People look at the settlement and think, "Oh, well, everything should be OK because he got this amount of money," but they don't understand so much about how that money is dispersed. In Rodney King's case, a large portion of that money went to the lawyers and medical bills. He had to have reconstructive surgery on his face because the police actually broke his face in so many places. He had to pay out of pocket for the medical treatment of his ribs, shoulder, arm, and all of that. But what should have been part of the settlement was therapy for the rest of his life, and that wasn't even a thought even though it's so needed. I can go down the list of different survivors of police brutality that needed and suffered post-police terrorism. And it's a tragedy that such care is not provided. For me, speaking at these different schools and events has become a form of therapy that I desperately needed. I remember one event I was speaking at with Etan Thomas at Horace Mann School in Queens, and during the Q&A one of the students asked me if I felt I would ever be able to forgive the cop, Daniel Pantaleo, for killing my father, not because he deserved forgiveness but so that it wouldn't harm my spirit. I have of course been asked about forgiving Pantaleo before. For some reason, the media always asks family members of victims of police brutality if they forgive the cop who murdered their loved one, and it's such a callous and insensitive and cruel question to ask just so you can write the headline and tell everyone this victim's family member forgives this cop, but this was different. The student didn't ask if I forgave Pantaleo now. And he wasn't asking so that I would create some type of restitution for Pantaleo or absolve him like I'm a Catholic priest or something. The student asked if I would forgive Pantaleo so it wouldn't harm *my* spirit, and nobody had ever asked me that before. I told him and the entire audience that I was working on it. I wasn't there yet. Pantaleo hasn't asked me for forgiveness, he hasn't shown any remorse, and he hasn't been punished. And while I was saying that, the look on the young boy's face said to me that wasn't his point, so I told him that I'm not consumed with hate and a vengeful eye-for-an-eye mentality or anything, but my heart is broken because I no longer have my father with me. But as I was answering his question, I'm on stage really having an entire therapy session of my own because I had never really explored that topic before. Young people ask the best questions. I remember at another event, a young person asked me if I was getting therapy and shared after the event with me personally that she asked me that during the Q&A because she was worried about me and gave me a big hug and said that I was an inspiration for her. I told her that, honestly, I was still trying to figure this all out but talking about it does help.

Those speaking engagements, especially with young people, really became beneficial to my entire growth process.

CHAPTER 4

The Huddle

My father was killed on a Thursday. The first time we went to the National Action Network was that Saturday. And the following week, Rev. Al Sharpton had a march on Staten Island. I took the train and the bus to the march since I didn't have a car at the time, and when the march was over I was looking for a ride back to Harlem. Rev. Sharpton told me to get on "the Huddle bus," so I asked his daughter Ashley if I could ride the bus with them, and she welcomed me with open arms. On the ride back uptown, they told me what they do at the Huddle and how they meet every week and how it's a place to talk and get the support and guidance that I will definitely need moving forward through this process. So I took them up on their offer, and every Monday I would find my way to the House of Justice and attend the Huddle.

That was the first experience with therapy that I feel actually helped me. I had a safe space to express my real feelings, whether they were anger, sadness, frustration, whatever the emotion was, and I wasn't being judged for it. They actually told me that it was OK for me to feel whatever it was that I was feeling. Nobody had ever told me that before. The other therapists while I was in the foster system always told me how I should feel or what my emotions should be. But at the Huddle, they started off by saying, "Literally whatever emotion you are feeling right now is what you need to feel right now, and it's OK."

I remember telling them how much of a trigger it was for me to see the video of my father's death and how whenever I am doing an interview the media would want to begin the segment by showing the video. I understand because that's how they introduce the segment, but they don't think about how traumatizing it would be for me to see that over and over again. Sometimes I would close my eyes and hum so that I wouldn't be able to see or hear it if they would play it, but after a while I would get into arguments because they insisted on playing the footage. I asked them if they could add it in later if it wasn't a live segment, or I asked if they could not show the video because it was painful for me to see. Some media outlets actually took issue with me requesting that. They almost copped an attitude like, "We have to show it," so I started walking off interviews and getting into arguments with newscasters. And I didn't care who you were or what station you were on, it didn't matter, you didn't have the right to traumatize me especially after you called me for an interview—it's not like I called you. So at the Huddle I learned that it was OK for me to feel that way.

I was being literally tortured. Everywhere I went, people were talking about it, whispering, "Hey, that's Eric Garner's daughter." They were giving their opinions of what my father should have done. Bringing up my father's past, which they always do when someone is murdered by the police. When I went out, I would see and hear all of that. I don't know if my hearing got better because I could clearly hear every single whisper, whether I was on the train or the bus or walking in the street—so much so that I didn't really like to go places because it felt like everyone was talking about my father and looking at me, and the Huddle again told me that it's perfectly fine for me to feel like that.

I was really struggling for a while. And I kept having nightmares replaying what happened, seeing the cops' faces standing around watching, the people driving by, nobody helping him. It played in my head over and over again, almost like a movie because I could see all of the characters. I used to wake up completely drenched in sweat, or wake up crying so hard my chest would be hurting, and I have asthma so waking up to an asthma attack because the anxiety and torment from my dream, or should I say nightmare, was retraumatizing me while I slept. So when I woke up, I would just be sad for the rest of the day. For a while I was scared to go to sleep. Like the old-school Freddy Krueger movies when they would be doing everything they could to stay awake because they didn't want Freddy to get them, that's how I was afraid of going to sleep for a while because I didn't want my thoughts and my nightmares to get me, and that's the part that people don't know about.

So let me explain what the Huddle actually is. It's a weekly meeting at the House of Justice run by Rev. Sharpton's daughters, Ashley and Dominique. They bring in young people every week and teach them and guide them about the movement. They teach them about protesting, educate them on the strategy and effectiveness of protesting from a strategic standpoint. They teach them how to plan and organize. They educate them about what is going on in the community and different issues—businesses that have done something offensive and need to get called out, or if a business needs to be boycotted. They teach them how to properly protest. Also, they support different organizations and provide scholarships and send young people to college. This is all stuff that a lot of people don't know about, but I have seen all of the people, especially young people, who this benefits.

So at first, going up to the Huddle, I'm going to be honest, it was tough, because I didn't trust anyone. I'm just meeting them, and they expect me to share in a group how I'm feeling, with these people who I am really just meeting? And listening to other people's stories, at first, was retraumatizing. They were further along in their process of therapy, so they were speaking about it so freely. Using words like "murderer" or "killer" or describing what happened to them and I just wasn't there yet.

I remember one conversation about hate and how people feel toward their particular killer, and I told everyone that I didn't hate all police. I had police in my family. But I did have PTSD almost like a war veteran who comes home and jumps at loud noises. So anytime I would hear a siren, I would jump. Actually, I still do at times. Some hip-hop songs had sirens in them and I would always jump even though I was familiar with the particular song and I know the part that has the siren in it, but I still jump. Same thing with flashing lights. And in the city, you hear sirens and alarms and noises and flashing lights literally all the time, so I was in a constant state of jumping and being startled.

I also feared that if I ever did need the police for any type of help or assistance, once they saw that I was Eric Garner's daughter they would refuse to help me. I felt that if I was ever in a situation where I needed to call the police, I would literally reach out to anyone for help before picking up the phone and dialing 911. That I definitely felt. I didn't trust the police to actually protect and serve me if I needed them to. I was also surprised to hear so many people not only say again that they not only understood what I was saying, and that I had a right to feel that way, but many of the people agreed with me. They were also so traumatized that they would call the police as a last resort and never a first one, and that's the complete opposite of how it's supposed to be.

CHAPTER 5

Rev. Sharpton

When I first met Rev. Sharpton, his focus was on my mother and my grandmother, and I was kind of in the background. So the family had a relationship with him, but I really didn't. Of course I knew who he was, but besides just being briefly introduced to him we didn't have a relationship.

After a while, I had just been dealing with a lot. I left Payless because it was overwhelming when people recognized me. I needed a job where I could be low-key and just busy myself so I wouldn't be constantly thinking of everything. I needed to focus on a job that wasn't going to bombard me with more trauma, and my mother was helping me look. Then about two to three weeks later, we were at a march with the National Action Network, and Rev. Sharpton came up to me and said, "Hey, your mother told me that you were looking for a job," and I told him I was, and he looked at me, smiled, and said, "Well, Monday you can start working at the House of Justice." He told me that he had reviewed my resume and that I already had a lot of skills and talent and that what I didn't know they would teach me. So the first thing

Rev. Sharpton did for me was give me a job. And I really enjoyed my time working there, and I really appreciate Rev. Sharpton for giving me that opportunity. I worked there for about a year. The job was great and I was learning so much and the people there were great, and after a while I wanted to go back to school, so Rev. Sharpton actually continued to support me and my daughter Kaylee financially while I was in school. He never told anyone about that. He could've broadcasted it to make himself look good and say, "Oh, I'm financially supporting Eric Garner's daughter while she's in college, I gave her a job at my office," but he didn't do any of that—even as people who don't know anything slander him as if he's only in this to make money for himself. Rev. Sharpton didn't have to do any of that for me. While I was in college, I was able to get to a therapist and get what I needed for my mental health without the financial burden that would have brought along more stress, anxiety, and struggle so I could focus on pursuing my academic goals. And everything was on track before my sister passed.

After that, I took her kids and had to go to court, deal with ACS (the New York City Administration for Children's Services) and so on, so I had to put my academic pursuits on pause, but even with that, Rev. Sharpton supported me. Because there were times where I was like, "What am I gonna do with three kids? I can barely handle my own daughter, now I have three kids? How am I going to do this?" I knew I was going to take care of my sister's kids, but I didn't know *how* I was going to take care of my sister's kids, if that makes sense. And Rev. Sharpton was right there to encourage me and let me know I could do it and reassure me that it's what my sister would've wanted, and that I was doing the right thing and that they would help me with whatever resources I needed. I felt like he was in it with me—and not just financially but emotionally. He encouraged me which was so important because many times it felt like the weight of the world was on my shoulders.

Then when my grandmother got sick, I was struggling with three kids, and my grandmother came to live with us while she was in hospice. Rev. Sharpton saw me struggling to keep it all together, and he paid for a nurse to come and help tend to my grandmother while I focused on the kids. He didn't have to do any of this. He had done enough for me and my family. He told me that he said he would be there to support me in everything moving forward, and he did just that.

Rev. Sharpton has supported me to the fullest, and I am forever grateful to him for that. He went above and beyond his call of duty. So when people are out here criticizing him, I always tell them that they have no idea what they are talking about, because if he truly was who they say he is, he would not have helped me the way he always did. I know the people who were trying to exploit me, and Rev. Sharpton was not one of those people. I remember when we were at First Corinthians Church in Harlem, and we were having a panel discussion and memorial for my father. I was launching my foundation, and Rev. Sharpton came as one of the speakers. This wasn't part of the script, because we were just going to announce that I was starting my foundation and that I would be doing a lot of work to honor the memory of my father, but Rev. Sharpton said, "No, while we have all of these people in the community here who love and support the Garner family, let's do a fundraiser." And I remember I looked at Etan Thomas and Pastor Mike Walrond who were comoderating, and they looked at me like, "Well, if Rev. Sharpton wants to go off script. . ." Rev. Sharpton said he was going to start the donations off and donate a thousand dollars himself, and he encouraged everyone else to support me. I was blown away. Again, our plan was just to announce that I had a foundation, but Rev. Sharpton was supporting me to the utmost just like he said he would.

People would come to me all the time and warn me about Rev. Sharpton and have nasty things to say about him, but one thing I noticed was that it was always something they heard, it was second- or third-hand information, and never what anyone had personally experienced. People have told me about negative personal experiences they have had with other people I won't name, but not Rev. Sharpton. People are always repeating what they heard. And I can say that just wasn't my experience with him. Rev. Sharpton went above and beyond, and he encouraged me to come to him anytime I had a question or issue about anything. His door was literally always open to me.

Another thing people say is that Rev. Sharpton just wants attention and to be in the media, and I tell them that that's what we need, and what he does is put the police on blast for things they've done. I explain to people that many people, especially in New York, would never have heard about my father's death and hundreds of thousands of other cases if it weren't for Rev. Sharpton. It's important to remember that he was doing this before social media became a thing. He was doing this when all he had was his bullhorn and his track suit, and he knew that if he made noise, the media would cover the story and that's the only reason we even heard about so many of the police brutality cases that we heard about. It's easy to take Rev. Sharpton for granted now in the era of social media, where news of police beatings and murders can spread like wildfire, but social media hasn't been around that long, and for a long time so many cases would have been kept quiet and out of the public eye if it weren't for Rev. Sharpton in particular. People shouldn't forget that.

CHAPTER 6

My Sister, Erica Garner

My sister, Erica, and I had a normal sister relationship growing up. There was a sibling rivalry at times. My mom didn't really let us go outside a lot. In Brownsville, Brooklyn, at that time, there were a lot of bad things going on. Drugs, crime, kidnappings, and my mom didn't let us just go around willy-nilly. That wasn't the program in our house. That's just the way it was. So we spent a lot of time inside. In fact, we were called the window kids, because we would sit in the window and watch the other kids play outside and have fun and enjoy themselves while we were stuck in the house. All we did was get into things. We were a little destructive at times, breaking things and making a mess. We were kids inside with nothing much to do. We played video games, played with our toys, watched TV, and ate.

In school, my sister was the overprotective big sister, and I was the sickly kid, because I had asthma. I was always in the nurse's office, always in and out the hospital, always sick. So for a while, Erica was like, why is she getting so much attention, why is everyone always so worried about her. But then if anyone ever messed with me or talked bad about me, she was the first one there to take care of business for me, and Erica didn't play. She was tough and always had the fighter's spirit. Few words were needed, she talked with her fists, and people got the message. Kids can be cruel and like to make fun of people. So me breathing hard, or being out of breath, was a target for jokes at school, but Erica was having none of that. A lot of people didn't mess with me because they were scared of Erica.

My sister was a tomboy. You know the song, "Anything You Can Do, I Can Do Better"? That was Erica. She would challenge the boys to basketball, climbing trees, slap boxing, whatever. I wasn't doing none of that. Plus, with my asthma, I just sat on the side and watched and was prissy, and she would peek at me making sure I was good while kicking the boys' butts in whatever they were doing.

She was my big sister, and we may have argued with each other like sisters do: "Stop wearing my clothes." "Why are you hogging the TV?" "Stop faking, you ain't sick at home." But once we stepped out of the house, she protected me.

So fast forward, and she had her daughter, Alyssa, and I had my daughter, Kaylee, so the girls grew up together. They were cousins, but they grew up like sisters. And when my father was killed, I was twenty-two, Erica was twenty-three, my daughter was two, and Erica's daughter was about to be four. And we were all very close.

About a week or two before my father was killed, him and Erica had an argument. I don't remember what it was about, but they never got the chance to make up and apologize. They had arguments before. We all have arguments with each other, and time goes by with people being mad at each other, sometimes a little bit of time, sometimes a lot of time, then you make up and you move on. Well, with them and this particular argument, they never got the chance to make up because he was killed, and that hurt Erica to her core. She would always say that she never got a chance to say she was sorry, she never got the chance for them to hug it out and go out to eat, which was their routine. No matter what happened, our father would always welcome us back with open arms, with a big smile and his big bear hugs and tell us it's OK. Even when we both were in our rebellious teen years, thinking we were grown and that we knew everything and would pop off like teenagers do, he would never hold a grudge, he would always forgive us.

I remember calling my father when I got pregnant, and I was like, "Daddy, I don't know what I'm going to do. I'm so sorry, I know this isn't the way you wanted it to be. You wanted me to be married first, and you warned me to be careful." And he responded, "It's OK, we'll figure it out." I remember one time calling him because I was struggling and didn't have any food, and I thought I was grown and living on my own and wasn't going to ask anyone for help. He didn't say, "I told you so." He just said, "Don't worry, I got you." That's who our father was. I could call him for anything. He would say that he had no problem with us trying our way first, and if it didn't work to come to him and he would take care of it. And he always did.

So going back to Erica, when he was killed she really needed bereavement counseling. She was a daddy's girl, our father's first daughter, and she was so connected to him and vowed to get justice for him. It became her everything. Nothing else mattered in life except getting justice for our father, but she couldn't balance. It took over everything. She wouldn't eat, she wouldn't sleep, it was all the uphill battle of fighting for justice. And it didn't matter if she didn't have the support. She would be there by herself protesting if nobody wanted to go with her that day. Just her and her megaphone. She was on a mission, and nothing else mattered. Her main focus was for the police department to fire Pantaleo, and she wanted the grand jury minutes. Those were her two main points.

For some reason, there is a law in New York City that nobody can see the grand jury notes—section 50-a of New York's Civil Rights Law. I'm not sure why, but that's the rule. And since they decided not to indict Pantaleo, Erica wanted to see those minutes, and she wanted section 50-a to be completely repealed, which would have allowed her access to all of the notes, evidence, and proceedings that led to them deciding not to indict Pantaleo.

The National Action Network really gave her a lot of support throughout this entire process. They were there with her every Tuesday and Thursday, which were her protest days, and they really did a lot with her as far as support, marches, protests. They really had her back, and Erica was just going nonstop. Like I said, it took over her entire life. And because there was no counseling and there was no therapy, everything started to go left for Erica and for the entire family during this process. We all started to splinter apart. And Rev. Sharpton tried to bring us all together: I remember one time he had us all in his office—me, my sister, my brothers, my mother, my aunt, my grandmother, my father's sister—and he explained to us that in times of trauma such as this it's important that the family sticks together because it's easy to splinter apart. And he told us how the media will pull us apart and pit one family member against the other and put out headlines of one family member saying something that contradicts another family member, and how the stress and trauma itself can pull family members in different directions. He told us that he's seen it happen so many times and for us to be careful that it didn't happen to us. Unfortunately, we, and I'll say we as a whole, didn't heed his advice, because what he warned us of was exactly what started happening from that point on.

My father had always been the voice of reason and the peacemaker in the family. And now that he was gone, there was nobody there to put the pieces of our family back together. So not only did the police kill my father, they killed the structure of my family.

But back to Erica, she is dealing with this nonstop and fully engulfed in justice. She didn't care about anything else, any issues within the family or any other aspect of life. Her only purpose for living was to get justice for our father, and it was taking its toll on her physically, mentally, emotionally, spiritually, every way possible. It was starting to break her down, .and I could see it because she's my sister and I was connected to her. At one point I had to tell her, I said, "Erica, stop watching the video!" I took her phone and said, "You're torturing yourself. This isn't healthy. You have to stop!" Anyone that knew my sister can tell you that's something you would normally get punched out for doing—snatching her phone, telling her what to do, nobody did that to her. But I loved her and would run the risk of a beatdown to get her to hear me and to save her because I could see what she was doing to herself. And I remember after I snatched her phone and told her to stop watching the video, she looked at me with tears in her eyes and said, "I can't." That's when I really knew how much she was struggling.

After a while, Erica and I started working together, and she wanted me to do all of the paperwork and let her do all the talking, which I was perfectly fine with. I didn't really want to talk and be at the forefront. That was more her personality. So we started working together. She really wanted to pursue children of the movement (the concept and pillar of my organization—children who are in the movement, a place where we discuss trauma, mental health, and healing through panel discussions, workshops, and protesting). After we did a panel with Etan Thomas and a lot of other NBA and WNBA players, like Swin Cash, Jerome Williams, and John Starks from the Knicks, who my father absolutely loved, Erica was really gung ho about connecting with other children of victims of police brutality and trying to help each other—that was going to be the goal.

In the midst of all of the planning, we found out Erica was pregnant with my nephew EJ, and she was having a lot of issues with the pregnancy. So I offered to take care of my niece Alyssa while she worked through that difficult pregnancy. The baby was born in August, and Erica started to have issues with her heart starting in September. She went into cardiac arrest twice after she had the baby. After she came back, I helped her out by taking Alyssa and helping take care of the baby as much as I could.

Around Thanksgiving that year, I heard she was walking around with a defibrillator to monitor and regulate her heart because she was having heart issues. And I remember telling her, "You have to take care of yourself, you have to do whatever it is that you are supposed to do to keep calm, take your medicine, eat right, you have to do it." And I remember her telling me that she had nightmares about them killing our father, and it was haunting her every time she went to sleep and how sometimes she didn't want to sleep because she couldn't stop the nightmares. And the fact that Pantaleo was still walking around free like nothing happened, living his life with his family, was literally tormenting her. I didn't know what to say because I was experiencing the same thing. I just pleaded with her to take care of her health and her heart because we needed her to be there, and her kids needed her, and the family needed her, and I loved her and needed her to be there. And she kept saying, "I'll be fine, we have bigger battles to focus on, I will be fine, don't worry about me."

Then, on Christmas Eve, my neighbor knocked frantically on my door and let herself in with a key I had given her in case of emergencies. I had turned my phone off and was going to sleep. I knew I had a lot of Christmas stuff to do the next day. So my neighbor is banging on the door and comes in and says, "Emerald, it's your sister, she had a heart attack, she's in the hospital and she didn't wake up." She then handed me her phone, and it was my mother, and she said I needed to get to the hospital right away.

So I get to Brooklyn from Harlem, and it's around three o'clock in the morning, and the doctors tell me that they're working on her but she flatlined in the ambulance and she's in a coma, and my heart just sank. I was actually in denial of what the doctors told me. And when they let me go see her, I came in there talking to Erica like she wasn't in a coma. I said, "Come on, Erica, we have things to do. It's Christmas. You gotta get up, we have things to do. If you can hear me, squeeze my hand." But she didn't respond, and she didn't squeeze. I just didn't want to accept or believe that my sister wouldn't pull through this and be right back protesting and marching and fighting for justice probably the day after Christmas because that was her. She was a fighter, she was a warrior. She was my personal protector and a part of me was devastated that I couldn't protect her as I looked at her in the hospital bed in a medically induced coma.

So after that, the doctors told me they needed to run tests and do a full-body CAT scan. She didn't get a lot of oxygen to her brain, but they were able to resuscitate her. They had to do a procedure though and nobody could visit her for twenty-four to forty-eight hours.

On December 26, my brother got a call from someone my sister used to work with saying the cops raided Erica's hospital room and were going through all of her stuff. My questions were, "How did the cops get access to her room, and she is not conscious? Why would the hospital let the cops into her room, and what are they looking for?" She went to the hospital in a nightgown so didn't have anything in the hospital, what is it that they're looking for. And they didn't find anything and nothing was released to the public about this, but we never got the answer of why they were in the room in the first place.

Then, a few days later, the doctors told us that Erica wasn't going to make it through the night.

On December 28, I brought Alyssa to the hospital so she could say goodbye to her mother, and we both said our goodbyes. The doctors told us they saw some brain waves and that was a good sign, so I was hopeful. When you have someone in the hospital in a situation like that, you will cling to any glimmer of hope, it doesn't matter how small or what the chances are. So in my mind I was thinking, Erica is still fighting and she's going to make it.

The next day, the doctors tell me that if she does make it out of the coma she will need help walking again, talking again, and I said, "No problem, we'll figure it out. That's my sister, so whatever she needs I will be there for her. She can live with me, we can all be a little community, my kids her kids, and we'll make it work. I just want her to be OK."

When I get to the hospital the next day though, they walk me into this conference room, and I'm looking around like, "What is going on, just yesterday you told me she had brain waves, she should be OK, and this looks like a movie, what is going on?" So the nurse sat me down, and I could feel that she was going to give me some bad news, and before she even said anything I broke down crying. They told me Erica had another heart attack that night, and I needed to tell my mother and all of the family that my sister had lost too much oxygen to her brain, she was not improving and she wouldn't make it through the weekend, her organs were going to shut down one by one, and the best thing they could do was make her presentable so that everyone could see her one last time and she would be gone by Monday. Then the nurse proceeded to tell me that the reason she is telling me all of this is because she viewed me as the strongest one in the family and she thought my mother and grandmother wouldn't be able to handle this news, and she liked the way I handled situations with the family, like when my grandmother was upset and when this person was upset. I'm thinking to myself, "Honestly, thanks but no thanks. I didn't ask to be put in this situation. And I don't know why people keep saying I'm so strong, I need comfort myself, and you're telling me my sister isn't going to make it through the weekend and you want me to deliver this news to my whole family, on my birthday?" Because it was my birthday that day. And she hugged me. So I had to tell everyone. I lifted all of the visiting restrictions and told everyone to say their last goodbyes.

I went to Erica, said my goodbye, and told her that I would take care of her kids and not to worry. And I told her I loved her and thanked her for being a wonderful big sister.

Then on December 30, I got the call and I didn't even answer the phone. As soon as I saw my phone ringing repeatedly, I knew that Erica was gone.

◊ ◊ ◊

Daniel Pantaleo didn't only kill my father. The mental, emotional, and physical aftereffects of my father's death also killed my sister. So he is responsible in that sense for the deaths of both of them. There's no doubt in my mind. Erica never had any heart issues prior to my father's murder. In fact, she didn't have any health issues. I was the one with the asthma problems. Erica was perfectly fine, and I could visibly see the change in her after our father was taken away from us. I found her diary after she died, and the stuff she was writing in there was mind blowing. She was tormented daily by what happened to our father. She died asking the question, will we ever get justice? And it ate away at her soul and her entire being.

She was the lioness of the family, she was the one who pushed for the New York City Civilian Complaint Review Board (CCRB) to have a trial. And if it weren't for her, they wouldn't have had a trial.

They had already ruled not to indict Pantaleo. Erica didn't get to see Pantaleo even be fired. He was still active on desk duty, walking around free and acting as though nothing happened, when Erica died, and it hurts me to my soul that she never got to see even an ounce of justice from all her hard work paying off.

In 2017, Erica was on *Democracy Now* speaking to Amy Goodman and said, "I've protested. I've spoken on panels. I've traveled across this nation. I've exhausted all avenues. I've even endorsed Bernie Sanders to get my message out. And we keep having the conversation I have exhausted for two years. How much talking do we need to have? The Black Lives Matter movement has been very compassionate, patient, and has basically been begging the nation. We are under attack as Black people. We're being gunned down every day, and these officers are not being held accountable. No charges, from Tamir Rice to my dad to Freddie Gray."

There have been so many times that someone has come up to me while I was out with the girls and said something to the effect that the police killed my sister, or they believe the police went into the hospital like they did on the movie *Judas and the Black Messiah* to the other Black Panther who was in the hospital, and killed my sister. And they say it right in front of my niece. There have been a few times that I had to get loud with people in the middle of a restaurant or at the park and tell them, "Why would you say that to me? And her daughter, my niece, is literally right here with me, and you say something like that in front of her? How insensitive is that?"

Everyone knows I took her kids, and it's so interesting because people think I have her lawsuit, my lawsuit, all this money in the world, and it's just not true. I'm struggling. I've never stopped working since my father was killed. I've always had a full-time job and then activism came second. But while I'm working, everyone thinks I have all this money and they don't think I deserve or need anything. It's so interesting how so many people can be so confident in facts that they do not have.

CHAPTER 7

Fire Daniel Pantaleo

After my father was killed, I was working for the New
York City Administration for Children's Services. I
was a case aid, so I had to transport children to vis-
its. My main location was on Staten Island, and I would see
Pantaleo as I would drive through Staten Island. Sometimes
it would be in an unmarked car, looking at least to me like
he was on active duty when he was supposed to be on desk
duty. I also know people in Staten Island who said they were
either stopped or arrested or given a ticket by him in particular inside of those five years when he was supposed to be
on desk duty. His face was all over the news, so it's not like
people didn't know what he looked like or like he could walk
around incognito or anything. Everyone knew exactly who
he was.

One day in particular, I remember driving with my
coworker in the agency vehicle, and a car was coming toward
me, and I saw him and looked right in his face for a few seconds because we were at a stop. Wiping my eyes and shaking
my head to make sure I was seeing what I thought I was
seeing and it wasn't someone who just looked similar to him,

but no it was definitely him. And I had a full panic attack. I was hyperventilating and the whole nine yards. My mind went in all types of directions. "What if he recognizes me? I need to be able to defend myself because I can't let him just kill me like he killed my father. What should I do?" Could you imagine the torture of living through those types of experiences where you come face-to-face with your father's killer? That happened quite a few times, and it was torture.

I didn't even like to drive past the street where my father was killed. It was traumatic every time I would see that street. I would take a long route and be stuck in traffic just to avoid that street. But to have to see Pantaleo walking around free, not a care in the world and still working as a cop as if nothing happened, hurt me to my soul, and I was going to dedicate my energy to pushing for justice for my father the way my sister dedicated her entire life to that before she passed.

So, Pantaleo had remained on "desk duty" since the murder. My sister Erica had been protesting tirelessly throughout the entire time he remained employed after killing my father. She protested in front of the police station where he was on desk duty. And in Harlem I was participating in protests and marches across the Manhattan Bridge. We were doing marches and protests all around New York, and it was that pressure that we put on New York City that ultimately led to him being fired. We didn't let up. It's almost as if they thought we were going to grow tired and fizzle out and give up after a while, but we kept applying the pressure. We kept trying to get someone to step up and do what's right—Mayor Bill de Blasio, the police commissioner, anyone who could hold Pantaleo accountable. They kept telling us to wait for the federal government to do it, wait for the Justice Department to bring federal civil rights charges, and they kept having all of this faith in the federal government, and as we saw the federal government decided not to even indict Pantaleo, and that's when I lost it. I exploded on all of the people who read the decision to us. They made us wait five years and then came back with a decision they could've made in two weeks. If it was going to be a no, they could've said no two weeks after my father was killed.

So we continued applying pressure, including by putting pressure on the mayor, who was somehow trying to keep us calm and tell us to trust the process the entire time. That's what he kept saying to us: "Justice will prevail, the system will work." But we were tired of waiting. I called for eleven days of action in 2019, the same day that the federal judge handed down the decision not to indict Pantaleo. This is the day we lay on the ground in front of One Police Plaza, the day we marched across the Brooklyn Bridge and did a lot of press, I did over one hundred media hits, discussing what was going on, standing with other families, to keep applying the pressure.

I remember being contacted by Change.org, which was where I started my petition "Fire Daniel Pantaleo." I let everyone know that with this petition we were going to go to the federal government and keep pressing for them to reverse their decision or to at least fire the officer. We got over one hundred thousand signatures, just an amazing out-pouring of support, and the police commission backed down and Pantaleo was then fired—not indicted, which is what he should have been, but at least fired. So after five long years of protests, marches, demonstrations, let downs, disappoint-ments, waiting, hoping, and praying, Daniel Pantaleo was finally fired and stripped of his pension benefits.

The New York Police Department judge who recom-mended that Pantaleo be fired said Pantaleo was "untruthful" and that his account of my father's death was "implausible" and "self-serving." But the question that still remains unanswered is why did it take so long for them to reach this decision? And what exactly led the federal government not to indict Pantaleo? What exactly did they investigate? How can one judge come to the conclusion that Pantaleo was "untruthful" and "implausible" and the federal government come to a different conclusion? Did they not see all of the evidence? And why did the federal government choose not to indict?

So many people dropped the ball with this. We protested in front of Gracie Mansion, where Mayor de Blasio then lived, and I asked him myself why he wouldn't stand with us publicly. He supported us privately and behind closed doors, but he would not publicly come out and say to the world that Pantaleo was wrong and needed to be fired, and all of the cops who were present and participated directly or indirectly, and allowed or didn't stop Pantaleo from choking my father to death were wrong as well and should all be charged. That's what I wanted him to say publicly, and he kept saying he couldn't do that and that we should "trust the process" and the federal government would bring justice, which it did not. Being fired is not justice. Pantaleo being indicted, charged, and sentenced to prison time would be justice.

In fact, I believe Pantaleo should be retried as a civilian. Since he is now fired, he wouldn't have all of the protection of the police, the union, all of the laws that protect police, and hurdles you have to jump around would be taken away. It would be him being tried as a nonpolice officer. I think we would get a federal indictment if that happened because the courts would look at him differently. The courts view police as innocent until proven guilty. That's just the way the system is constructed. But with civilians, we're typically considered guilty until proven innocent. I know that's not how it is supposed to be, but in actuality that's how it is. So, since he is no longer a cop, he should be tried as a former cop, a fired cop, and I am convinced the outcome would be different.

Just look at how Patrick Lynch, the head of the NYPD union, vehemently defended Pantaleo after he was finally fired after five years. They were ready to storm the castle. They held this big press conference and stood there in front of an upside-down NYPD flag and condemned Pantaleo's firing. He said:

> It's absolutely essential that the world knows that the New York City police department is rudderless and frozen. The leadership has abandoned ship and left our police officers on the street alone, without backing. . . . There is no confidence in the leadership at city hall and One Police Plaza. We are following up that with a call to the governor, to have the mayor removed from office for malfeasance and nonfeasance. He abandoned his post. He refuses to do his job. And has joined the antipolice rhetoric that we already know got two police officers killed. And now has caused the street to disrespect our uniform and the women and men wearing it.

He was basically saying, how dare you fire my good, clean, wholesome officer for killing that person who didn't deserve to live. That's what he was saying. They wanted the mayor's head on a platter. Go back and look at the actual video. He is so angry and irate. Veins all popping out of his neck. And all of the police officers standing behind him.

New York police commissioner James P. O'Neill announced his decision to finally fire Pantaleo and these were his words:

> The unintended consequence of Mr. Garner's death, must have a consequence of its own. Therefore, I agree with the

deputy of commissions of trials legal findings and recom-
mendations, it's clear that Daniel Pantaleo can no longer
effectively serve as a New York City police officer. In carrying out the court's verdict in this case, I take no pleasure.
There are no victors in this decision made today. Not the
Garner family, not the community at large, and certainly
not the courageous men and women of the police department who put their own lives on the line every single day
to service the people of this great city.[1]

Now, my reaction when hearing this was I was completely offended. I couldn't believe what I was hearing. He
was acting like some great tragedy had occurred and he was
sad for Pantaleo—not sad for my father who was killed but
sad that Pantaleo no longer had a job. He expressed regret
and somehow acted as if this was a sad day for the New York
City Police Department. He didn't stand against this type
of behavior or say, "This is not what the New York City
Police Department represents," or, "We want to improve the
relationship between the police and the community or reassure the community that we want what's best for you." He
expressed regret that Pantaleo would no longer have a job.
His entire address was not aimed to express regret for my
father, it was solely to express regret for Pantaleo. Don't get
me wrong, this came as no surprise to hear this from him, but
it was offensive nonetheless. He never once throughout this
entire process reached out to my family and expressed regret
for my father being killed. In fact, the only contact we had
with him was indirectly during the CCRB trial, when he
sent word to us that my mother's crying during the trial was
disturbing the court and that he wanted her to be removed.

The police were so disrespectful during the entire proceedings. They were laughing, arrogant, loud in the hallway,

telling stories of apprehending criminals like they were in a bar or something. Their statements on the day of my father's death did not match the testimonies they gave in court.

I often think about the other policemen who were present during my father's murder. The ones who stood around and didn't intervene to stop Pantaleo from choking my father to death, the ones who didn't have the decency to step in and say, "OK, he's down that's enough," the ones who just stood there while my father said he couldn't breathe eleven times. I believe they should all be fired and brought up on charges. But what a lot of people don't know is there is a reason they weren't brought up on charges, and that is because they were all given immunity. There was a strategic decision made by the NYPD to have it all be placed on Pantaleo. I'm not sure why they made that decision, but that decision was clearly made.

This is why we wanted to repeal section 50-a of the New York Civil Rights Law. We wanted all the transcripts from the trial to be released because we wanted everyone to see what we saw—the contradictions, the cover up, the falsifying statements, the failure to report and follow proper procedures, the outright lying. We wanted everyone to be able to see all of it.

I'll give you an example. There was an officer who said on the day he got to the crime scene that Eric Garner was unresponsive, and then he sat there in the courtroom that day and said he was fully awake, that he was aware and up. But even though they have a record of him saying that he was unresponsive when he got to the scene, because he received immunity, there were no consequences for him. So him and all six or seven other policemen who were there that day received immunity, and that is criminal in itself.

CHAPTER 8

The Eric Garner Law

I had the pleasure of speaking with so many different people as I continued on my quest for justice. One of the people who helped me tremendously in 2020 during quarantine was New York state senator Brian Benjamin. As we were revving up to embark on this battle, I asked Senator Benjamin if I could interview him so we could have documentation of us getting ready to do something monumental and have a long-standing impact on the entire country. He agreed, and this was our conversation detailing our plans to bring about the Eric Garner Anti-Chokehold Act.

BRIAN BENJAMIN. Emerald, how are you?

EMERALD GARNER. I'm good. How are you?

BRIAN BENJAMIN. Listen, I'm just working hard, and I'm just glad to be here to help. I've been dealing with police reform issues. One of the things that we talked about the other day is, the governor signed this executive order saying that localities have to reimagine policing in their neighborhoods and their communities and people have to provide a report of how they're going to reimagine and rethink about policing or else there won't be any state money. So I've been trying to start talking to folks, thinking about what does that look like? I need you and folks who are most impacted by this system having this conversation on the floor when we're making these decisions, otherwise it's not going to work. We can't have people who are thinking about this theoretically making decisions on what's happening to our impacted families. So I'm glad that you and I are talking right now.

EMERALD GARNER. Yes. I'm super glad about it. As I said before, I never felt like I had a seat at the table. I just felt like I was just going with the flow, and now I'm knocking doors down. You can't keep me out of the room now. I want to be super hands-on involved, because I feel like enough is enough. Like, you know, something has to happen, something has to change. So that's why my push as soon as I heard of everything with George Floyd, I was just like, you know, you murdered another one of our brothers, and you still haven't passed the chokehold law. So if the chokehold law was in place nationally, then these cops would be facing up to fifteen years in jail. And that's just the bottom line.

BRIAN BENJAMIN. That's right. So it's in the bill, the bill named after your father. It basically says that if, unfortunately what happened in your father's case was the police acknowledged that a chokehold was put on your father, but because the chokehold was not criminalized in the law they were able to get off. So we said, "You know what, you're not going to be able to do that again." We've now criminalized it. So if a police officer does a chokehold on a civilian, they're looking at up to fifteen years in prison, and that's your father's bill. And you know, we're going to make sure that gets implemented and we're going to keep on going. We're going to take this nationally, as you and I talked about. So I'm very excited to be your partner on this.

EMERALD GARNER. Yes, absolutely, let's take this nationally because when I first started talking about this, I was like, "OK, make this a federal law." You got to go through channels, and I'm not a politician. I don't know about the channels and the networks and stuff. That's why you're here to explain to me like, "No, Emerald, you just can't do it that way. It's just not going to happen that way. There's you know, there's checks and balances." So you have to work out those types of things. And what I'm working on with Senator Gillibrand and Senator Warren is presenting it on a federal level, so I need elected officials like you and Natalia Fernandez and Michael Blake. I need all of the elected officials to come together. I'm willing to go to every single state, get in my rental and go to every single state and talk to every elected official about presenting this in their state so that they can get this law passed because if it was passed in New York State, it wouldn't matter when George Floyd was murdered because it's only passed in New York. So the fact that the officers were fired immediately and that they were charged, that's nice, but we need them to be convicted. We need them to serve jail time.

BRIAN BENJAMIN. That's right. And we've got fifteen other states. Well, fourteen other states outside of New York that have Democratic governments, the legislatures and their governors. And we want to make sure that those states have no excuse. They can't say they got a Republican or Trump or nothing like that. They got no excuse. So we want to work with them, and we want to make sure, like, I'm sure some of those states, we've got people who are carrying the bill, and there are people like me in those states who are carrying the bills. We want to go and sit down with them. We're going to talk to them. We're going to let them know that they got all our support. We're going to help them with funding. You're going to come down there. If you got to protest, beat someone up, whatever.

EMERALD GARNER. Whatever it is, I'm calling everybody out.

BRIAN BENJAMIN. So, I'm excited that you have asked me to be a partner, and you need more partners. I'm happy to be one of your partners, because I believe we should come coalesce around you and help you rise and take this forward. You know, I know sometimes the families that have lost a loved one, you know, sometimes they get pushed out of the way for other people. And I don't believe in that. I want to pour into you and facilitate your leadership and rise. And I will be, you know, a support member as you do what you got to do, because you are the right vision for police reform across the country. And so I need to help you do what you need to do on behalf of all of our people.

EMERALD GARNER. Thank you. Yes, absolutely. one of the things that I've been working on, which is you know, a lot of people don't know this, but I do formal conversations. I do open forums. I've been to multiple colleges, including Harvard, Yale, Howard. I've been to UCLA four years in a row. I do a lot of speaking, and I built myself up to be better at public speaking. When I was young, I was in the Respect Project. I got a lot of poetry and spoken word underneath my belt. For me, Erica was the politician. Erica was the one that was taking herself into a world of politics. I was like, "Erica, I'll be your personal secretary. I will answer your phone calls. I will dress you. I will do your hair. I will be in the background." Now that she's not here, that strong leader voice is not here, I can only be half as good as she was and hope to be all of what she was when she was out there. Because, pandemic or not, Erica would be out there yelling and screaming, and I would be at home with Alyssa as well. So it would be this way either way.

BRIAN BENJAMIN. Tell me what you ideally want to have happen here. Like what would make you feel like this was time well spent? I feel good about what we accomplished. What comes to mind when you think about that?

EMERALD GARNER. When I think about what would make me feel at ease and what I would consider to be justice, it's carrying the chokehold bill nationally and making it a federal crime. Also, along with the other two pieces of legislation that we had in the national call, which was the Andrew Kearse Act where you have to give medical attention. Because even if we had an act like the Andrew Kearse Act, my father would have gotten oxygen. He's a known asthmatic. He had an asthma pump outside his bag. If you're searching someone and they have an asthma pump, that tells you they have asthma. So putting their arms behind their back and jumping on them is not good for somebody who has asthma or any type of respiratory issues. For Andrew

Kearse to die the way that he died, now there's an act that says, you have to give medical attention, even something as small as that would have saved my father's life. I do believe so because, during the video (I watched it during the CCRB trial, I never watched it beforehand, I only watched clips), the EMT workers were talking to him as though he was alive and "you'll be OK, it's all right, you're on the way," but you're talking to him, but you're not helping him. So with that little piece of legislation, the Andrew Kearse Act, that would have been like, "You're going to jail. You don't give medical attention and you're a medical professional you're going to jail." That's the bottom line. For me, taking it nationally and having young people see that this is an injustice. This happened, but we don't have to sit down and take it.

I've been saying the era of a child that needs to be seen and not heard is over. All of these young people are undecided. They don't have any leadership. Look at the president. Forty-five is not giving them any hope. The president is not giving them any guidance. And that's why they're out here in the street wilding out. I don't blame the looters for what they're doing. They're stressed out, they're fed up. I don't want them to be out there doing that. I don't want them to be out there looting, but they're not guided, they have nothing to do. We need to give these young folks something to do. We took away some of the youth programs because of the crisis, because of the pandemic.

So what are we going to do with these young people? Now is the perfect time to get them involved in organizations, get their voices heard, and find out what they need. Let's find out what the young people need in their communities. Because what I see is a lot of young people walking around and they have nowhere to go. The community center closes at eight. Some kids can't go back home until ten o'clock, because their parents or foster parents tell them you can't come back home until it's time for your curfew. Unfortunately they're left out there. My ultimate long-term goal, where I see myself in ten years, is having a twenty-four hour community center. Some type of an organization set up where I can give around-the-clock help, to even the small people, not just people who are mainstream in the media, not just people who get the media attention, because there are other people that don't want the media attention.

BRIAN BENJAMIN. That's right, that's absolutely right.

EMERALD GARNER. They don't want it to be national because then they become a target. I'm definitely afraid. I'm afraid that I will be assassinated when I speak out about police brutality. That's a fear of mine, and that has nothing to do with experience. It has nothing to do with my life. It has everything to do with the murder of my father, because of my name. I'm afraid to call 911. I'm afraid to call paramedics. I'm afraid to do those things because I'm speaking out against them. Are they going to help me? I want to ease the minds of the young people, because they probably feel the same way that I do. Maybe it's just made up in my head. Maybe that's just a mental illness that I've developed after my father, but who knows. We need to focus on the mental health and physical health of the young people coming up, because we want to encourage them to be police officers. Not say, "Oh, you know, we don't like cops." And then they don't want to become police officers. We need to police our own communities and that's what I see long-term.

BRIAN BENJAMIN. And we want to get rid of bad policing, you know? So, one of the things you mentioned was Andrew Kearse, so, the governor signed the bills. So now most bills have been passed in New York State, which is phenomenal.

EMERALD GARNER. Awesome, that's a victory!

BRIAN BENJAMIN. Yes! And we're going to work together. We're going to also bring in Sister [Angelique] Kearse and we're going to take this like a package right across the country.

EMERALD GARNER. Yes. It's a package because, with that, and even with the Stephon Clarke Law we entered, when we did the national call, we wanted to present three pieces of legislation because what happens, though, in most of the encounters is you're either shot, choked, or denied medical attention. And that's mostly what happens in the death of a victim. We're calling ourselves survivors. My sister didn't survive the movement, but I did. I'm going to be presenting those three because although my father was not shot, he was still killed by a police officer, so with the Stephon Clark Law you are not allowed to shoot anybody in the back as they're running away from you, as our young brother in Atlanta, that just happened to him. If a law like the Stephon Clark Law was passed in his state of Atlanta, Georgia, and where he is that officer, OK, he's arrested for first degree murder, but under the Stephon Clark Law, you shot that person in the back, that's a federal crime and you're going to federal prison.

With those three things, that's what's going to make people think, "I'm going to shoot you in the back. Nope, better think again. I didn't think about that really because I'm going to lose my job, lose my freedom, and lose my pension. Lose my money, lose my house, lose my family." And that's what they need to be thinking about because Angie Kearse was left with no husband and four kids. Four young kids. She had seven kids in total, but she's left with four kids under the age of ten with no support. My father passed away and then my sister passed away. Her kids were left with no support, no mother, the fathers are not involved. They only have me to depend on. I have to make sure that I keep myself together. I keep my mental health together. She also has to make sure she keeps her mental health together. She has to keep her family together. And they really don't know the effect that they left on the family. Like, "You murdered my father, you took away our head of the family and now we're ultimately suffering." So, you know, I'm appealing to everyone. You know, their moral compass, because if you see a video of my father and you still say that federally Pantaleo should not be charged, there's something wrong with you.

BRIAN BENJAMIN. No, no doubt about it. And I think one of the reasons why that bill was so important was because I don't want to get into what his intent was or what you thought his intent was. The bottom line is, you used an illegal maneuver and you killed an innocent man, you're going to jail, period. Part of our conversations. We want to take all the discretion out. We don't want to start talking about, "Oh, well, did he intend to do it? He was just trying to constrain them." False, none of that stuff should have happened in the state of New York or anywhere else in this country. So we're going to work on making sure that we get that done. And so what we need to do is we need to come sit down, come to the office, sit down, let's go over the states, let's go over the people who are carrying the bills.

Let's start figuring out who are some of the people who are ready, existing allies that we might not even be aware of across the country. Get them on a call, have you talk about what you've been through or talking about what we want to do. And our office will basically help track all of it and help you take this thing nationally. But it's one state at a time. It's one cosponsor at a time, it's one chamber at a time, right? This is real work X's and O's.

EMERALD GARNER. Crossing my T's, dotting my I's like, I'm ready to get started on this like next week. I don't really know how to, I just Googled it. And I was just like Democratic states, and I just got a list. So I'm just looking at it and then I Google certain things that I want to know, of course, I'm going to send you emails with questions, "Hey, what does this mean? What does that mean?" I'm smart but I'm not a politician. I got a B in American government. I think that's OK. I think I know a little something something. So yeah, definitely. I definitely want to get the ball rolling. We have to do it. We have to get it done.

And I feel like, with this specific day, I say, "I wanted to have survivor-led conversations because a lot of the times the activists come in and it's just like, OK, well, sit down, we'll talk for you. I don't want anybody to talk for me. Not at all. I want to talk for myself." You know, I have something to say. I want people to hear me. I think the more that I talk, the more that these messages will get back to Pantaleo. Look what you did. You did this. If you didn't kill Eric Garner I would still be at Payless. I would probably be retiring by now. You know, you did this. So just know that this is what you did. This is a direct reaction to what you did. I did want to take some questions from people. I don't know if anybody has any questions. If you guys have any questions for Senator Benjamin, if he broke it down the way it needs to be broken down, we spoke about it in layman's terms. If you are a police officer, you are on duty, you arrest someone, you choke them to death. You're going to jail, bottom line. Under the Eric Garner chokehold bill we're going to be taking this national.

BRIAN BENJAMIN. And also it's not just choking. It's a chokehold or similar restraints. So anything that obstructs the air or to the throat or windpipe. So the knee to the neck that happened in Minneapolis, you're going to jail for that too.

EMERALD GARNER. Yes, the seatbelt maneuver that they were talking about at the CCRB trial, arm technique, all of it, everything.

BRIAN BENJAMIN. However you define it. You can sit on my neck, whatever it is that constricts that blood flow, you're going to jail, very specific. We wrote the law to make that happen. And that's the language we need to make sure it's passed across the country. Because if we don't do that, then you could be in a situation where we can't give the police any wiggle room. It's got to be very clearly stated. Quite frankly, the NYPD, at least in our case, it's illegal per the rules.

EMERALD GARNER. Yes, in their handbook it's a banned procedure. And you know, like I always say, in retail, you get written up twice, you're grass, you lose your job. I don't understand why there's a difference for police officers. I also want to figure out, you know with 50-a, I was talking to Jayshon and I was like, "Hey, so, since 50-a has been repealed, can we get the transcript from the CCRB trial as well as the police reports from 717, the day my father had died, along with all of the other evidence." Can we get that? Do you know if we can get that?

BRIAN BENJAMIN. I don't know that specifically, but we'll look at it. I think I saw a question that came out here. Can you read that question?

EMERALD GARNER. The law speaks about the police being charged with a class C felony, explain that.

BRIAN BENJAMIN. So, the way we did the bill was that if a police officer uses a chokehold or similar restraint that leads to serious physical injury or death, that would fit the criminal offense of aggravated strangulation, which would be a class C violent felony, which could land you up to fifteen years in prison. And so that's the class C, it's the class C violent felony, but the actual crime would be aggravated strangulation, which is a new crime that we created that is specifically tied to police officers. So right now you, if a person can strangle another person, that leads to serious physical injury and that's an offense already. We created an aggravated strangulation when a police officer does it, that leads to serious physical injury or murder that can land you up to fifteen years in prison. So the class C felony, this is a violent felony. It's under class C nonviolent felony. It's just how it's written in the penal code that has the sort of prescriptive. That means it must be this amount of time in prison, that's on the table.

EMERALD GARNER. I hope that explains it. That's definitely what we needed. We needed the language because I'll tell you, sitting in that CCRB trial, when they tried to play on words and talk in circles. I was just like, do you know that we can hear you?

BRIAN BENJAMIN. What they basically were saying was, "OK, maybe he shouldn't have done the chokehold, maybe it's not in the NYPD manual, but it's not a criminal offense. So you can't incarcerate him for that." So that's why we created this bill where the chokehold is a criminal offense. So just by doing it that you can be prosecuted for that and end up fifteen years in prison.

EMERALD GARNER. And that's what we want. We want prison time. We don't want just an arrest. We want jail. We want the officers involved, every single officer, not just one officer, because in my father's case, what they did was put everything on Pantaleo and gave everyone else immunity. And that's what we don't want to happen in the future. That's what we don't want to happen at all. We don't want anybody getting immunity. Everybody needs to go to jail, everybody involved. So if you're a "looker-oner" and I think we should come up with a bill about, you know, blowing the whistle on your coworker. We need to definitely come up with some type of legislation for that, because if you're standing there and your coworker is killing somebody, you should have the right to intervene.

BRIAN BENJAMIN. And Minneapolis has this too, which is why those other cops got arrested. We have in our law where you are required to step in as a police officer, we did that last year. So unfortunately we weren't around for your father either, but where if a police officer is doing something inappropriate, the police officers who are also there will be liable if they don't step in.

Accountability in the system, right? So this is for example, your father's law is the first law in the history of New York State, where a police officer committing a crime is now an elevated offense. Typically, whenever an offense happens to a police officer that's elevated, right? So, if I murder someone, it's one charge. If I murder a police officer, it's that charge plus, right. If I assault someone, that's one charge. If I assault a police officer, it's that charge plus you get more time. This is the time when we flipped it, where we said, if a police officer does something that is a bigger crime than if an average person does it. We said, we need to hold them to a higher standard. It's their job to protect and to serve. And so I think this reorganizes the culture, which I think is going to help. Let me give you a perfect example, look at Atlanta, that cop is being charged for murder, who shot Rayshard Brooks. That's brand new.

EMERALD GARNER. First degree murder.

BRIAN BENJAMIN. You know, well, they don't know. They got to think about it. Now cops are getting fired, so we have a long way to go, don't get me wrong. Pantaleo was on the job for how long? He was on the job for almost five years.

EMERALD GARNER. Five additional years after the incident, after the murder. Think what we have started to do is we're now finally holding police accountable.

BRIAN BENJAMIN. Five years after he killed your father! Progressive New York City. So we're just going to keep pushing this thing forward. We're going to keep pushing this thing forward. But I think to the question, we already have the laws on the books. It's just that they never applied in the force on police officers. So we just got to force that situation and that's where we can end up going. I'm happy to answer more questions if that works for you.

EMERALD GARNER. We can. What I wanted to talk about, because a lot of people are confused by this executive order that Trump just signed. We can close with that. I think a lot of people are confused because they think, oh, President Trump is on our side. Not just yet. Hold on a minute. Because for me, the words that bothered me were "review, police enforcement, excessive force," whatever. Once he said "review," I was like, "What is there to review?" You have Eric Garner, Mike Brown, George Floyd, Sandra Bland, you have Rodney King. You have all of these videos of people, countless videos of people being killed by police. So to say, "review"?

BRIAN BENJAMIN. An executive order is not a law. So you know, that could change the way. So executive orders are never usually the things you want to stress about. The way Trump wrote the executive order, there are wiggle room and loopholes in it that it makes it almost useless. But what he did do was be able to try to give some peace to some of his supporters who felt like, "Oh, well, maybe we shouldn't kill all the Blacks." You know what I mean? And so it's more optics than it's anything real. If he was serious, he would put forward legislation that could get passed that would actually execute specific things. He would criminalize the chokehold, like we did in New York State. He would do that federally and take care of that, whatever he's doing. So, you know, it's one of those things where it's a smoke screen, you don't want people to try and distract you. Don't get distracted, keep your eyes on the prize. Until we get him out of office. We're going to have to go state by state and get this bill passed, but let's get Joe Biden into the White House and force Joe Biden to do the right thing, and I think he will.

EMERALD GARNER. I think he will. I honestly do think he will. You know he stood behind the federal Eric Garner chokehold bill. He's definitely one of the supporters. Shout out to Kirsten Gillibrand, Elizabeth Warren.

BRIAN BENJAMIN. I think Hakeem Jeffries carried it in the house.

EMERALD GARNER. Hakeem Jeffries, yes, of course, absolutely. And, you know, shout out to everybody who's carrying it. You know, thank you so much for giving me the space, giving me the time. I look forward to what we're going to do next week. After Tuesday, I'll be available to come and we could talk and set up things. I've been doing my little research on my end so we could just meet in the middle. So thank you so much.

BRIAN BENJAMIN. Thank you.

EMERALD GARNER. Yes, we're going to make it happen.

◊ ◊ ◊

It took the NYPD five years to find that Daniel Pantaleo did in fact violate a departmental ban on chokeholds. So many people ask me, "Why did it take five years? If the chokehold was already banned, what was the discussion about? Why did you need a new law to be put into place for something that is already banned?" Well, let me explain.

Lawyers of the NYPD began changing the language they were using when describing the murder of my father. They stopped using the term "chokehold" when describing what Pantaleo did and began saying he performed a "seatbelt maneuver." A chokehold is defined as "any pressure to the throat or windpipe that could hinder breathing." Now, mind you that the New York City medical examiner ruled my father's death a homicide, let me make that clear. For a while they were attempting to say that my father died from cardiac arrest and not the actual chokehold, but the medical examiner's official report concluded that he died from "compression of neck (choke hold), compression of chest and prone positioning during physical restraint by police." The medical examiner did report that contributing conditions were "acute and chronic bronchial asthma; obesity; hypertensive cardiovascular disease," but he reported in his conclusion that it was in fact a homicide, meaning those contributing conditions are not what killed my father, it was the chokehold that killed my father.

NYPD Commissioner Bill Bratton publicly promised to retrain all NYPD officers, but I seriously doubt they ever had any real intention of actually carrying out that promise because, again, the chokehold was already banned since 1993 for all NYPD officers. This isn't a new discovery, it has been "prohibited" for a long time. In fact, a year after the ban went into effect, an NYPD officer killed a twenty-nine-year-old man named Anthony Baez with a banned chokehold after Baez's football hit a cop car.

Three days before my father's death, another NYPD officer was caught on video using a banned chokehold on Ronald Johns, a twenty-three-year-old man who was allegedly caught trying to enter the subway through a service gate. The video depicts brutal footage of Johns being held in a chokehold and beaten by an NYPD cop. This was all on video because a civilian pulled out her phone and recorded it.

There was another incident where Rosan Miller, a twenty-seven-year-old woman from Brooklyn who was seven months pregnant, was put in a chokehold by an NYPD officer for "illegally grilling."

There are countless more examples I can give, but my point in giving these is to show that their "prohibited," "banned," "frowned upon," or whatever they want to call it, chokehold has been regularly utilized by NYPD officers all around New York City in broad daylight since it was banned in 1993. And something needed to be done about it.

Now, back to my father and the disciplinary trial for Pantaleo. His defense attorneys have maintained from the start that he used what's called a seatbelt maneuver, which is approved by the NYPD and differs from a chokehold in that it involves putting an arm over a person's shoulder and not around their neck. But after being shown a still photo taken from video footage, Deputy Inspector Richard Dee concluded that Pantaleo was, in fact, using a chokehold.

Here was Mayor de Blasio's official statement:

> On behalf of all New Yorkers, I extend my deepest sympathies to the family of Eric Garner, on this day we have received the Medical Examiner's findings concerning the cause of his death. My administration will continue to work with all involved authorities, including the Richmond County District Attorney, to ensure a fair and justified outcome.

We all have a responsibility to work together to heal the wounds from decades of mistrust and create a culture where the police department and the communities they protect respect each other—and that's a responsibility that Commissioner Bratton and I take very seriously. I've said that we would make change, and we will. As Mayor, I remain absolutely committed to ensuring that the proper reforms are enacted to ensure that this won't happen again.

I'd also like to thank the Office of Chief Medical Examiner for conducting a thorough and expeditious review of the cause of death in this tragic incident.[2]

Mayor de Blasio said during a Democratic presidential primary debate in 2019 that he knows the Garner family personally and that there will never be another Eric Garner because they are changing fundamentally how they police. At that point, we didn't know him personally, and he was greatly overstating his interaction with us. I understand it was for political reasons, but he didn't have to say he knew us personally. We hadn't even spoken at that point. I remember later sitting in a meeting with him and he didn't even know my mother's name. So I found it interesting that he sat on that stage and told the world that he was close to Eric Garner's family and knew us personally. If you don't know his wife's name and his children's names, then you don't know the Garner family. To say you know the Garner family because you met his mother is not knowing or being close to the Garner family. But don't use our name and pretend to support us when you didn't. I feel that if he was really committed to us, he would've fired Pantaleo right away. He claimed that he wanted the federal government to do their job. And when the same federal government who he had so much faith in, who he told us that would bring justice, dropped the ball and chose not to indict Pantaleo, I personally asked him about it and he did nothing. I was so tired of people paying lip service—people who had the power to actually do something, only supporting us with their words but not actions.

Now, at that same presidential debate, there was Kirsten Gillibrand on the same panel who said, "If I was the mayor, I would fire him, but as president I will make sure that we have a full investigation, that the report will be made public, and if I wasn't satisfied, we would have a consent decree." She was amazing. She called out Bill de Blasio for his inaction and told the world that he very much had the power to bring action and fire Pantaleo had he chosen to. She made it plain. And she is someone who didn't just support us behind closed doors, or make very nice-sounding public statements, but actually used her power to do something.

She reached out to me to tell me that she was working on the federal legislation to present the bill not only in the state but also federally. And that bill would make chokeholds a federal crime. So we had a national call and requested all of the New York State Senate to join the call. And the stipulation of the call was, "If you don't join this call, you don't support this cause." So we had an amazing call. We discussed what in particular we needed to do in order to get the law passed. We discussed what support we needed, how many signatures we had to get. We examined the amount of support and signatures we had gotten at that point along with Change.org and we strategized on ways to get more support, to get people to publicly support the bill, support the law, and to support Eric Garner, and how that would increase our chances of getting a federal legislation.

Elizabeth Warren was also someone who gave us a great

amount of support. She let us take over her social media to spread the word about the Eric Garner law, to educate people on why it was important to ban chokeholds for all police, and to explain how they were trying to differentiate the "seatbelt maneuver" from the "chokehold" with my father and how it's all really the same thing and should be illegal. She had national calls with us and updated us on what was going on with the Senate and what we needed to do next. So she was extremely helpful.

Speaker Carl Heastie and assembly member Walter T. Mosley announced the New York State Assembly passed the Eric Garner Anti-Chokehold Act, which would criminalize the harmful use of a chokehold by a police officer. Assembly member Walter T. Mosley said in a statement:

> Almost six years ago, we heard Eric Garner tell police "I can't breathe" as he was put into a choke hold by an NYPD officer. His words now speak from the grave as we deal with the police killing of George Floyd under nearly identical circumstances. Hundreds of unarmed Black men and women have been killed at the hands of police officers before and between these two tragedies. In 2015 I introduced this bill to outlaw chokeholds statewide, and I am proud to see it taken up today as we pass legislation to reform our criminal justice system. This is an important step forward, but it will not be the last. We must work to change the way that police officers interact with communities of color, or we will continue to see these killings occur.

Speaker Carl Heastie said, in support of the bill:

> I have worked with my Assembly colleagues to reform our state's broken criminal justice system. Holding law

enforcement officers accountable for their actions is a necessary part of that. The NYPD ban on chokeholds was not
enough to protect Eric Garner, and it is not enough today.
This legislation will put an end to the practice across the
state.[3]

On June 8, 2020, both houses of the New York State
Assembly passed the Eric Garner Anti-Chokehold Act. Let
me explain why the Eric Garner law is so important not just
in my father's case, but moving forward for all police across
the country. The act criminalizes the use of chokeholds, or
aggravated strangulation, of any kind by police officers in
the state of New York. The act "would occur when a police
officer or peace officer obstructs breathing or blood circulation by using a chokehold or similar restraint thereby causing
physical injury or death to another person. This would be a
class C felony, punishable by up to 15 years in prison." This
was huge! I cried like a baby when they passed this because
this meant that the police could no longer do what they did
with my father and attempt to change the terminology and
say they were using a seatbelt maneuver and not a chokehold
or arm hold or arm technique, because anything that restricts
the breathing of someone now constitutes a chokehold and is
punishable with jail time.

The New York City Civilian Complaint Review Board
(CCRB) reported 996 allegations from people who have
reported that the police have used a chokehold on them
between 2014 and 2020, even though the New York Police
Department banned the use of chokeholds in 1993. But it
was never criminalized before, and that's the difference. It
was frowned upon but not illegal. That's what kept Pantaleo
from being fired initially, because it was frowned upon but

not illegal. And now, the NYPD will never be able to use that defense again, so all of our hard work and fighting and pushing and marching and calls was finally paying off.

But we're not satisfied. Right now we are at a point where it is going to be presented federally, and we're hoping to get this federal bill passed. If this law were federal, Derek Chauvin would've been indicted under the Eric Garner law immediately because kneeling on George Floyd's neck for over nine minutes would be considered an illegal obstruction of breathing or blood circulation—not frowned upon or against their policy but actually illegal. And we are not going to stop until we get this passed federally. My sister would be so proud right now. Although we didn't get prison time for Pantaleo, we were able to make a change.

CHAPTER 9

When We Feel Exploited

At the 2021 Grammy Awards, Lil Baby's performance of his song "The Bigger Picture" began with a reenactment of police shooting a Black man and featured Tamika Mallory, an organizer of the 2017 Women's March and an affiliate of Rev. Sharpton's National Action Network, speaking about the nation's "state of emergency."

Tamir Rice's mother, Samaria Rice, responded to this performance in a series of Facebook posts: "I'm tired of you black lives matters (Tamika Mallory and crew) bitches that's riding theses family back and yall ambulance chasing Attorneys (Ben Crump) (Lee Merrick) too yall have fuck up our fight and yall can kiss my ass too. . . Yall might as well be junior pigs cops." Samaria Rice also released a joint statement expressing many of the same criticisms with Lisa Simpson, whose eighteen-year-old son, Richard Risher, had been killed by a Los Angeles Police Department officer in 2016. They called on Tamika Mallory, Shaun King, Benjamin Crump, Lee Merritt, Patrisse Cullors, Melina Abdullah, and the Black Lives Matter Global Network to "step down, step back, and stop monopolizing and capitalizing our fight for justice and human rights." In their words,

> We never hired them to be the representatives in the fight for justice for our dead loved ones murdered by police. The 'activists' have events in our cities and have not given us anything substantial for using our loved ones' images and names on their flyers. . . We don't want or need y'all parading in the streets accumulating donations, platforms, movie deals, etc., off the death of our loved ones, while the families and communities are left clueless and broken. Don't say our loved ones' names period![4]

In an interview with Imani Perry, Samaria described how, in the weeks after Tamir's death, various people offered Samaria Rice guidance. "You can see I look like a deer in headlights," she said of early interviews. She told Perry she was angry but had been told she wasn't supposed to show her rage, that she felt constrained and underinformed, and that she didn't want the organizers and lawyers to "handle everything." She wanted to be involved in strategy, court filings, and decision-making.

Perry recounts how Tamir was killed while "playing with a toy gun, as so many boys do," across the street from his home. Someone called the police, reporting the gun they said "was probably fake" and that the person holding it was a juvenile. However, upon arriving at the scene, Officer Timothy Loehmann hopped out of his car and shot at Tamir twice "without warning, while his patrol car was moving."[5]

It was almost like something out of a movie. I myself had never seen a policeman do that in real life. How the entire world could see the video of that execution and the cop still not end up behind bars was a question that troubled many in the country. He was a child playing in the park! Protests spread across the country. The national media began to run stories on the incident, and the world was introduced to Tamir's sweet face. Comparisons to Emmett Till and Trayvon Martin were made more and more. And the public found out that neither officer at the scene performed first aid on Tamir in the minutes after he was shot, and Timothy Loehmann had been declared unfit for duty due to his emotional instability, but Cleveland police hired him without reviewing his file.

Of course impacted families are not a monolith, and we all have different ways of coping, especially in that initial time frame after the tragedy. Some don't have the mental or emotional capacity to be involved in any decision-making or legal strategies, and others feel differently. It's a time where you don't know who you can and cannot trust, who is trying to exploit you and who actually cares about your well-being, who talks a great game when the cameras are on about justice and being for the family and who is just trying to use you because the spotlight is on you in that moment.

I have personally experienced my share of all of that, as have many other impacted families. The truth of the matter is that not everyone who puts their hand out to help you is actually trying to help you. And it hurts to find out anyone isn't who they presented themselves to be.

There is no script to follow or way you can prepare yourself for this whirlwind of a moment, of people tugging at you from every direction. Some telling you to control your emotions in front of the camera while others are telling you to show your emotions in order to create empathy. We become global figures, not even national but global, but the reason you are global is because you are now a part of a group that nobody on earth wants to be a part of. You're a part of the "my family

member was murdered by the police" group, and nobody who
has never been in that situation knows how that feels. Even
if you feel compassion, empathy, rage, or whatever emotion
when you see the picture of the person who was killed, and
even if you feel a connection to that person, you will never
feel the pain that their mother or daughter or wife or son or
brother or sister feel, and people need to remember that.

Samaria Rice's public lashing out understandably offended
those she called by name, and Mallory, King, and Abdullah
responded publicly. The activist community was divided.
Some were siding with Samaria Rice while others were siding with the activists. I think everything Samaria Rice said
was out of years of frustration and feeling exploited. Let me
be clear, I am not choosing sides in their dispute. I've come
across many activists, including the ones mentioned. I have
done panels with Shaun King. He has never raised money
on my behalf, and when we reached out to him to speak at
my father's memorial he came and spoke and didn't ask for
an honorarium. He has also supported my sister, but beyond
that I cannot vouch for or condemn Shaun King in any way
shape or form. Same for Tamika Mallory. I have heard other
survivors say different things about their dealings with both
of them, but I have never had either of them raise money on
my behalf nor have I worked with them beyond Shaun King
speaking at my event, working with my sister, and attending
her funeral.

Now, that being said, I would never discount Samaria
Rice's feelings or experiences. Nobody knows how she feels
except her. And everyone grieves differently. And her experiences could differ from my experiences. And everyone has
a right to feel how they feel. People don't understand how
it feels to feel like your loved one is being exploited after

they are murdered by the police. And we all have felt that at one point or another in some form or fashion. Like I said, I've definitely felt it myself. And let me just say, speaking from experience, it's a terrible feeling to have. Imagine losing your loved one and fighting for justice for years, still not having justice for your loved one, no resolution, your emotions are all over the place, and you see people move from one story to the next and you're still looking for justice for your loved one. People don't understand that survivors are left with that pain and that hurt and there is no moving on to the next story. We're still stuck. For me it's still Eric Garner. For her, it's still Tamir Rice. For Sandra Bland's family, it's still Sandra Bland.

So it's a constant battle in deciphering between the people who are trying to help you and the people who are trying to exploit you. And sometimes, you confuse the two. I know I have. I have viewed people who I really thought were trying to help me and it turned out they were just trying to use me to better themselves, raise their platform, or even make money for themselves and their organizations. So I've seen it all. So no, you're never going to hear me bash any survivor for expressing their hurt and pain at what they perceive as exploitation, because I know how that feels.

But also sometimes activists aren't intentionally disrespecting, they just didn't ask the person what would be the best way to help them or involve them, which in my opinion should always happen. Everyone grieves differently and everyone wants a different type of assistance. There is no one way for all family members who have lost loved ones to police violence. That's just not how it works. Everyone is different. And if you reach out to them, they can tell you how best to help them and what they need.

You gotta understand, OK, so using myself as an example, I see "I Can't Breathe" literally everywhere—on The Chi, in the song by H.E.R., I see it everywhere. On one hand, it's great because these people are raising awareness, but then you see a shirt company print shirts that say "I Can't Breathe" and sell thousands upon thousands of shirts and they're actually making money off my father's last words, and my family, not even just me directly but my entire family, is not even included, so that hurts like you couldn't imagine.

There are levels to this. And in looking at some of the activists, nobody knew you before you started to build your platform solely off talking about victims, and then we're not included as well? Going back to the Grammys, Lil Baby is Lil Baby whether he does a song talking about everything that's going on or not. Killer Mike is an OG, he's been in the rap game forever, he is going to be Killer Mike whether he says my father's name or not, but sometimes it feels like some activists are solely making their name off our loved ones.

Now for me looking at the actual performance, I thought it was great. I saw it and thought that's wonderful they are bringing this issue to this big platform, and I'm sure there are a lot of people watching this who would rather not hear about this but we are bringing the issue right to them. Like Kaepernick taking a knee during their precious football game and national anthem. We are bringing this issue to you so you don't forget it.

But I have to honor how Samaria Rice took it as this is my son, and y'all are talking about my son and I'm not the one standing on stages talking about my own son. I wasn't even invited to participate with you while you are talking about my son on this big stage. I'm still here grieving, in pain, struggling to put back the pieces of my life. And you're being flown to perform at the Grammys to talk about my son and be praised for talking about my pain. I can't discount that feeling and nobody else should either. The system failed her and she has every right to feel however she feels about that.

Do I think it was malicious of Tamika and Lil Baby and Killer Mike? No I don't. I think it's amazing any time Black people stand up for Black people. But they have to understand that Samaria felt left out and she is in pain. Was her delivery a little harsh? Yes, maybe so. But they shouldn't even take it personally. They should understand and recognize that there is a lot of pain there that we as survivors are still dealing with no matter how many years have gone by since our loved one was taken from us.

You're talking about my dad over here on this big stage or platform, and I'm over here like, "Hey, I have something I want to say too." Why is your word about my father, or my son, or my daughter, more important than my word about them? I'm doing ten times the work you are doing. It became my sister's entire life, but we're not getting called to go speak at the Grammys, we're not getting called to speak all over the place, getting honorariums like you all do. And it goes back to again, why is you talking about our loved ones more valued than us talking about our loved ones. So that's where the issues arise.

But I thought this was a perfect opportunity for all of us, impacted family members and activists, to come together and discuss everything, put it all on the table, work it all out, and become a stronger united force within social justice. But a lot of people on both sides didn't see it that way. I tried too. But there was so much hurt and trauma that people couldn't even open their minds to the possibility of coming together. It was definitely a missed opportunity because we are much more united than we are divided. And many of these fights are uphill battles and we need all of the people we can possibly get.

Another topic that has come up from this is the issue of GoFundMe and Shaun King. So many people have asked me to comment on the accusations against him, everything Ms. Rice said, what other survivors have said, and I have chosen not to for many reasons that I now have the opportunity to carefully and thoroughly explain.

I have spoken to a lot of different survivors, and some have had good experiences with Shaun King and Tamika Mallory, and some have had bad experiences. If you speak to some survivors about Rev. Sharpton, I'm sure you will be able to find someone who has had a bad experience with him, but my experience was different, and all I can really speak to is my personal experience with someone. Shaun King never raised any money on my behalf and he has never done a GoFundMe for me, so I can't speak to anything concerning him and these fundraisers. It would all be hearsay. Now, that's not to discount anyone else's experiences with him because I would never do that. It is definitely possible for someone to have a different experience than I had, and that's why I have always refused to comment on this subject because people want me to pick sides, which I refuse to do.

My experience with Shaun King is that he had a good relationship with my sister and supported her, he came to her funeral after she passed, he spoke at my father's memorial at Canaan Baptist Church in Harlem and didn't ask for an honorarium or anything (which is good because we didn't have any funds to be able to give him an honorarium, so I was definitely thankful for that), and that's it. That's my only interaction with him. I see him bringing light to a lot of different cases, using his social media platform, speaking on different people's behalf, but that's all I know. So I'm not going to be put in the middle of anything that I can't speak with firsthand knowledge about.

So after this, another topic that came up was GoFundMe fundraisers and whether they should be set up for survivors or not. Now, as we all know, things get a little sticky whenever money is involved, so it is definitely a risk, but if it's done correctly and with the family being directly involved, not indirectly, but directly involved, fundraising could actually be a big help.

A lot of people took notice that after many cases where the police murdered an innocent Black man, woman, or child, and the cops were suspended (even though many times the suspension was with pay which isn't really a punishment but more of a paid vacation, but let me stay on topic), many times, that fired or suspended police officer would have a GoFundMe immediately raised for them and they would instantly have thousands upon thousands of dollars raised for them. So many people started to ask the question, what about a GoFundMe for the family members of the person who the police just killed. Where is their GoFundMe?

I explained how there is no counseling or mental health services for family when they go through the trauma of having their loved one taken away from them, how much that is needed even in my own family, and how much that money could be put to use. But it has to be done the right way. And the family had to be directly involved or things will get sticky.

In addition, where people drop the ball is where they send the money and where the money goes. I think if people are going to donate, they should do the research first and see if there's an estate set up. Is there an attorney? Make sure the money is going to the actual family and not being lost somewhere in the middle.

A lot of times, when we go and stand with organizations, because we don't have a nonprofit or anything set up like that initially, we are really just thrust into the middle of this whirlwind and people will send the money to the organization they see us standing with figuring that it will get to us, and that doesn't always happen. For us, we were with the National Action Network, and that's who people always saw us standing with whether it was marches or press conferences or actions or media. So when someone wanted to donate to the Garner family, they would send their donations to the National Action Network. Rev. Sharpton never told anyone to do that or directed anyone to do that, they just did it. But Rev. Sharpton, since he has been doing this for so long also has the proper system put in place to accept donations that come in and makes sure every cent goes to whoever it is intended to go to, and we have had no problems or issues with that. Unfortunately, not every organization has that same setup.

So what many of the survivors are saying is, as they are hearing from people that they donated to such and such organization that they saw standing with the particular survivor or raising money on the survivor's behalf and they didn't receive the money or didn't receive all of the donations, whether it's because they don't have the proper system in place or whatever the reason is, that's where the issue begins. And once that survivor is affiliated with that particular organization, they are able to maneuver and do things because of the affiliation. They get opportunities that they didn't have before. They are being flown around the world to speak on the topic of police brutality and activism and

saying our loved ones' names who we lost so they are bene-
fiting from our pain and suffering and we're looking around
seeing this happening while we are still grieving and still
suffering and still fighting for justice, a justice that many of
us will never see. So you have to understand when we lash
out. When we have had enough because we are still hurting
and grieving and in pain.

Now, of course, this isn't every organization and every
activist, let me be clear. Like I said, I have had nothing but
great experiences and support from Rev. Sharpton and the
National Action Network throughout this entire process, but
not everyone has had the same experience as me with other
activists and organizations, some organizations just don't
have the proper setup, and there are others who simply don't
do what they are supposed to do. That's the bottom line.

And sometimes, when some of us do get our foundations, 501c3s, and organizations together, we don't get the
funding or support that the other larger organizations get.
They have become household names throughout this process for their advocacy, but we are the actual ones hurting
and trying to make a difference and fighting for justice for
our loved ones and creating programming and writing
grants so that we can fight to ensure that what happened to
our loved one doesn't keep happening to other people, and
we can't get any support but rather people are supporting
the larger organizations who people recognize because they
have heard from them so much. So they are getting truck-
loads of donations and living good financially, and many
times we can't even get our foundation off the ground while
we are still grieving and fighting for justice. So again, you
have to understand where a lot of the pain and anger is coming from. After all of this happened, Etan Thomas told me

that a lot of different NBA players were asking him if they should be supporting the survivors or if they should stop saying their names, and I told him that NBA players and athletes and entertainers are different. They are not making their careers from us, they already have a platform, and they are using their platforms to elevate us. When Etan invited me to speak at his Black Lives Matter panel in Harlem after my father was killed, the event would have been just fine without my involvement. He didn't even ask me to speak. He wasn't trying to use me. He didn't even announce that I was going to be there or even announce me until I told him that I wanted to say something. That's different. I appreciate the athletes speaking on my behalf. Let me just speak for myself because I can't speak for all other survivors, and we are definitely not a monolith.

My experience is that after my father was killed, any time I would turn on the TV and accidentally flip past the news (I didn't like to watch the news because they kept showing the video of my father being killed over and over again), I would see people expressing what my father did wrong, talking about his past, his size, how the police officers were afraid for their lives even though it was seven of them and just my father by himself. I would see them vilify my father and ultimately express on camera to millions of people why they believe my father deserved to die.

But then, I saw these NBA players—Derek Rose on the Chicago Bulls, Kevin Garnett and a few of his teammates on the Celtics, LeBron James and Kyrie Irving with Cleveland, the Phoenix Suns team, Kobe Bryant and the entire Lakers team, all of these NBA players—wearing the last words of my father, and it really touched me. It was a direct contrast to what I had been seeing repeatedly on the news. It told me my father's life mattered, that what the police did to him was wrong. And they were showing up on their job and telling this to the world. I cried like a baby when I saw this. I was so thankful and so grateful, I wish I could give each and every one of them a hug and just tell them thank you, and all of my family felt the exact same way.

My father was a huge NBA fan. He loved his basketball, and he would've been so proud to see all of the NBA players wearing the "I Can't Breathe" shirts in support of him. I know this for a fact. And athletes already have their platform and their money, etc. They're not trying to exploit us, they are using their platforms to bring attention to our cause. I've been on panels with Etan and heard people say they paid attention to what was going on with Trayvon Martin after seeing LeBron and Dwyane Wade and all of the Miami Heat wearing the hoodies and talking about Trayvon Martin and how they would've just skipped past it if it weren't for them. I've heard people say the same thing about the Mike Brown case, the Tamir Rice case, my father's case, and so many more. Now, of course it shouldn't be like that. It shouldn't take an athlete saying this is wrong for people to be able to look at it and be outraged and say this is wrong themselves. But I understand Etan always urges current athletes to keep speaking up because people listen when they speak up. Admittedly, I didn't really get it at first, and I thought to myself why does he keep pushing for this so much? I don't care if such and such athlete says something or not, but now I get it. So I'm all about that push too. I definitely don't feel that athletes, entertainers, rappers, etc. should stop saying our names or stop advocating for us. We need all the help we can get. I would say that it would be great to involve a lot of us in your advocacy, which a lot of athletes have been doing, and that really goes a long way. And supporting our particular causes and foundations and efforts goes a long way as well, which many athletes have also been doing. Who am I to say don't feel sad for Eric Garner or don't say his name? I would never say that. Everyone saw the video, and everyone saw what happened. So I personally feel that anyone, no matter what profession they are in, who wants to stand up for my father, who wants to figure out ways to get Pantaleo indicted, who wants to find some way to hold the seven other officers who now have immunity accountable, who wants to help continue to bring awareness and attention to this issue, please do, and while you're doing it, just involve my family and support us as well in the process.

CHAPTER 10

Guidance from Lora Dene King, Daughter of Rodney King

I n the beginning, the media was all over me and my family. This was to be expected, although we weren't thinking about it at the time. Years later, people are still continuing to try and use our situation to benefit themselves in some way. Most recently, I had a difficult experience with someone I shall not name, who claimed they were using their connections out of commitment to the movement and out of love for me. Even though I initially believed this person, this was unfortunately a complete fabrication. This has been one of the more difficult parts of this journey, figuring out who to trust and who not to trust. One of the people I learned I could lean on for guidance and trust through this process was Lora Dene King, the daughter of Rodney King. This interview I conducted with her illustrates the nature of our friendship and the nurturing she has provided for me.

EMERALD GARNER. I just want to start by saying thank you and welcome to this very, very special episode of *Justice Pursuit* with Emerald Garner. I have here the wonderful Lora Dene King, the daughter of Rodney King. I've been anticipating this interview so much because we connected through a panel, and I listened to your story. I listened to everything that you dealt with and I heard similar things to what I went through. I feel like your story is kind of like, "What if my father survived?" I may have been telling the same story that you're telling right now. I just want to start by saying thank you. Welcome, I'm sending love and light to you. And I just want you to just give a brief introduction of some of the work that you're doing now, a little bit of history of stuff you've done before, and then we can jump right into our conversation.

LORA DENE KING. First I want to say this before I get started. I'm honored to be on this with you. And I too, I have the same connection with you. When I first got introduced to you over the phone when I was pregnant, you didn't know, but I was crying because I was talking like this [*covers her mouth*] and then I'll put the phone up because I didn't want you to know, you know how that is. I didn't want to project that energy on you. Each time after that, and when we did the panel, it was so emotional. I'm just honored to be here and I'm honored to call you my sister. And I'm honored to go through any journey that you need me for as well. Your strength, I learned so much from you just by being you. So I'm honored. I really am, seriously.

EMERALD GARNER. Thank you so much.

LORA DENE KING. My introduction. My name is Lora Dene King, I'm the middle child of the late great Rodney King. I'm also the founder and CEO of the Rodney King Foundation. There's a few, actually. I started the I Am a King Scholarship, which highlights African American youth.

EMERALD GARNER. Congratulations.

LORA DENE KING. Thank you so much. I started that two years ago to highlight African American men because the media does the opposite. They portray Black men as not great fathers, not great people, angry, upset. And I'm like, "Wait, I know plenty of dads. I know plenty of African American men that are amazing men." I always say what the media portrays, that's not who I know, and that's what they did to my father's character, to your dad's character, and we can go on and on with these hashtags.

EMERALD GARNER. Absolutely.

LORA DENE KING. That's not who they are, and I wanted to put it out there. This stemmed from the way my father was portrayed in the media and it hurt me to see. So I wanted to do this for his legacy and the legacy of all Black men. I wanted to tell the world that African American men are important. I know—and I say this, I'm a mother, so I can say this—a father's role in a child's life is the most important role because a girl learns her first love from her father and the boy, that's his example. We just wanted to highlight African American men and provide a great day for their kids and just fund a day out for a bonding experience and self-esteem time, because that builds so much self-esteem within our people and community. We feed the homeless, we do a thing called "one days of blessings."

EMERALD GARNER. That's great.

LORA DENE KING. Yeah, it's cold at night. And so we wanted to be a blessing to provide, you know, blankets, mittens, scarves, all those things, as well as COVID packages, as well as snacks and water, whatever we're able to provide for "one day of a blessing" to be a blessing because I know what it's like to be without. It doesn't have to be this or that, but I know what it's like to be without.

EMERALD GARNER. That's a great objective and goal.

LORA DENE KING. Right, right. We do yearly turkey drives. We pass out turkeys as well as box food. We do toy drives for children. We just did my dad's thirtieth anniversary of his beating in Imperial Courts, Watts, California, and we gave out five hundred hot meals to the community.

EMERALD GARNER. Congratulations.

LORA DENE KING. Thank you. Thank you so much.

EMERALD GARNER. That's all so amazing. I'm just sitting here in awe. That's a plethora of things that as victims we band together and do, and now we can definitely say that we're survivors because we came out on the other side of it. People have a lot of misconceptions of who we are as people. They tend to forget that we are people and that we have feelings too.

LORA DENE KING. You know, when I thought about this idea, I was just like, ah, every time I go on an interview, they want to ask me about the protesters. They want to talk about something that's negative. I had a protester ask me, like, if your father was white, do you think he would have been killed? I was just like, I really want to walk out of the interview right now, but I don't want to be rude. I wanted to still show some level of respect, even though I really felt like they were trying to disrespect me at the same time. When we met, we did our panels, we did our discussions and then we followed each other on social media, and I started to see the things that you do.

EMERALD GARNER. After we met, I definitely wanted to have to have further deeper conversations with you for so many reasons. Honestly, I needed it. The atmosphere of social justice has definitely shifted. We need more boots on the ground. We need more people to actually support us and follow through. We want to plan, organize, and execute. I know that you mentioned the media, this is the media, they will ridicule you. They will portray you in this negative light. I think my main objective now has shifted from, I know that I want to get justice for my father. I'm not staying on this side. I'm not staying on that side, I'm standing on the side of justice.

EWhen we talk about the media, we talk about what they say and what they do. My objective is to change the narrative. Now I want to create a platform where survivors are talking and then survivors are speaking and speaking truth to power and we're actually truly turning our anger into action. What is your experience with the media and some of the bad experiences, as well as some of the things that you would like to see change in the media and their portrayal of police brutality?

LORA DENE KING. I'm glad you brought up a point of pain. I've used this thing, I've used my pain to push me to my passion, because this is my passion to get justice, like you said. My thing is injustice anywhere is injustice everywhere. I feel like the media is tricky. One great thing about them is now as the whole world, let alone Americans, white America, Black American, Asian, everybody's forced to explain what happened to your father, the hashtag goes on and on. Now America has to explain this to their kids because these are innocent-minded kids. Their friends see it, social media posts on it, now they have to explain this to these kids. Before it was nothing, the kids are not exposed.

EMERALD GARNER. Now you can touch it. You can talk about it in school. You can't water it down.

LORA DENE KING. So, now they're forced to talk about it. I see more people, more nationalities speaking up in the media, it's tricky, it's really tricky. We have to bottle those energies because these are our fathers. People ask the most random things, I'm sure you get those questions too. I get my strength from my father when it comes to that, because I saw how he handled life. I'm like, "Who am I to be less than my ancestors, our ancestors, they went through so much, who am I to lessen myself?" Bottle up that strength and use your pain to push you. That's exactly what my pain does, push me.

EMERALD GARNER. Absolutely. That's what we're kind of forced to do. Before we were thrown to the wolves. We're regular everyday people. In your case, you were, how old were you when your father was beaten?

LORA DENE KING. I was seven.

EMERALD GARNER. You were seven. And then when he passed away, how old were you?

LORA DENE KING. I was twenty-eight.

EMERALD GARNER. Twenty-eight. When my father was murdered, I was twenty-two. I've had him my whole life, my mom and my dad, my whole life. Then my father was taken away at twenty-two. I had twenty-two years of memories. You had seven with a certain amount of memories, and then up to twenty-eight with a different amount of memories and a different type of memory. You have to keep reliving that. I bring up the media because when you have to keep reliving that you're reliving it over and over and over again. They tend to forget that we live in this. When this interview is over, we're thinking about everything. We're playing back everything. We're sitting there, we're thinking, did we say the right thing? Did we say enough? Have we done enough? Are we doing enough? It's always that self-consciousness. I just want to, like, say I appreciate you and everything that you're doing and I aspire to be as courageous as you and go head-on.

LORA DENE KING. You are, because I watched that video, I don't want to get emotional so I'm going to catch myself, but I watched it. I watched that video with you at the, I believe it was a police station, yelling.

EMERALD GARNER. Courthouse, the courthouse at the federal government.

LORA DENE KING. I admire you because you watched your dad get murdered. You get what I'm saying? At the time watching the video, I had no idea that was my dad. I thought, "Whoever this man is he's—I know he's dead." I had no idea that. . . So I understand, and for me, you're inspired by me? No, no, no. I'm inspired by you. The fact that you have to see that, that's a different kind of strength. You're here [*holds hand at a high point*], I'm here [*hold hands lower*]. You know what I mean? And it's like, emotionally, I don't know. I don't know if I could be as strong as you, because that's hard. I felt your pain when you were standing in front of there yelling, I was at home crying.

EMERALD GARNER. It was 2019 August. It was just such a battle-filled emotion because it was like, enough is enough. Nobody's hearing me. I got to stand out here and I've got to yell and scream and take my moment because nobody's listening.

LORA DENE KING. Right. I'm glad you said that earlier, the media can say this, that and that, but at the end of the day, these are our fathers. There's no right or wrong, because this is my life. This is my trauma. People ask the randomest things, I don't know. Proper etiquette doesn't exist.

EMERALD GARNER. It doesn't when it comes to the media. Etiquette doesn't exist in the media. That's why I feel like it's important for us to build our own platforms, control our content, control the narrative. A lot of people are hurt and use us as impacted families, survivors because of police brutality. However we label ourselves, I tend to forget that I am the story. If I don't want to talk about it, I don't have to talk about it. I have times where it's like, dang, I feel like I'm not out there. I'm not in the streets. I'm not hitting the ground running. But then either someone around me or I have to remind myself that I have done the work. I put in the blood, sweat, and tears, not because I chose to join this fight because I feel bad for an impacted family, but I am an impacted family who was thrust into this fight. I have a voice and I'm not trying to knock anybody off a pedestal. I'm just trying to create a lane, where we are seen as equal. I don't ever want to be a person to tear down another person. Even the people who have done me wrong. I never want to see you doing that. I never want to see anything bad happen to you, but we can talk about things. We can address it and we can move forward. Because at the end of the day, we're not on this side and we're not on that side. We're on the side of justice. We're all fighting for the same thing. And as we go forward, that's the mindset that we should have.

LORA DENE KING. Right. If we all close our eyes, who is that person? Not what you look like. And to me, that's real ignorance. You are judging somebody based off the color of their skin, that's true ignorance. You know what I'm saying? It's like, we're all part of this big puzzle. And without you, without me, the puzzle is incomplete. If we look at life like that, like we live in America, this is a golden opportunity, but is it? And my question to the world is, can we be equal? That's all we're asking.

EMERALD GARNER. Exactly. That's a big question. Can we be equal in the world where there's so much inequality? One of the worst questions that people ask me where it's just like, I feel like *Family Guy* where I'm like, "You know what grinds my gears? It just grinds my gears when people ask me, do you hate police officers?" That's the one question that the media just tries to get. Do you forgive the police officer? Let's start with, do I hate police officers? Absolutely not, I have police enforcement in my family. So I don't hate police officers. A police officer is someone who wears a uniform. You take the uniform off, you're still Paul, Peter, David, John. So you're still a person. It's all about your moral compass. It's about, are you morally competent to understand that when you sit on somebody it's going to stop them from breathing. When you choke somebody and they're telling you that they're struggling to breathe, you need to get off them. In order to forgive, you will have to acknowledge the hurt in somebody else. I just had a conversation with my friend, and we were saying that, in order to move forward, in order to start to heal, you need to confront the issue. You discuss it. You let the person know that this is how I feel. That person then validates, "OK, I understand how you feel. Maybe I didn't mean to say what I said or I didn't mean to say it how I said it." It's one of two ways that we can pick a side, agree to either move forward together or move forward apart. There's no bashing, there's no up and down. That's where we start with forgiveness. This officer never acknowledged, nor did he confront the issue and validate our feelings. No, we cannot move forward with forgiveness. Am I open to a conversation? Absolutely, that's how we have to handle it going forward. You are given three seconds to respond. That's the long answer, it wouldn't work.

LORA DENE KING. No, seriously you're right. I just don't understand it. It's like the other question they ask all the time, how do you feel about protesters and rioting?

EMERALD GARNER. What do you say about protesters?

LORA DENE KING. I don't, I'm not for rioting and every-thing. I understand that we need to get to the root of why they are doing that.

EMERALD GARNER. If you didn't kill us, they wouldn't protest. If you didn't kill us, there wouldn't be any riots. It's frustration, it's anger. It's hate, it's hurting, it's hurtful.

LORA DENE KING. It is wrong to ask that question. Last June they're saying it's a state of emergency. They're burning down everything. This is a state of emergency, but taking a Black man's life is not? That's disrespectful.

EMERALD GARNER. Storming the Capitol is not, some folks say they're just speaking out, exercising their rights. They're using their First Amendment. They're exercising freedom of speech. They're making a statement. When we protest outside of the Capitol, on the streets, we get permits. We organize, we plan, and we still get shot. We still get maced, we still get pepper sprayed. We still get hosed down. Truthfully, if you didn't kill us, we wouldn't have to fight for equality if there was equality in the world.

LORA DENE KING. It's like whupping a child, beating the hell out of a child and be like, "Don't cry. I'm doing this, I'm doing that, but I'm not agreeing with it, but I understand it. I understand where the hurt is coming from." If we get to the root of where it's coming from, then boom. But we're still here. It's ridiculous.

EMERALD GARNER. Absolutely. I'm so excited for the work that we're going to do together in the future. I definitely want to have more conversations. I definitely want to bring up more issues and discuss the issues so we can work together and do a lot of things. Conversations like this really help me. It inspires me and motivates me because I feel like you understand in ways that nobody else understands. When I talk to other victims, they can pull off different feelings. For instance, talking to someone who just supports the movement because they feel bad. To those people I say, don't look at me as a victim. I'm not a victim anymore. I'm a survivor and I'm going to come out on top. I have ideas. I want to fight in the social justice movement. All I'm asking is that you support me in a way that will help me elevate as opposed to helping me bring it down. I think that especially what you said about the media was spot-on because this is exactly what it is. We need to control the content and control the narrative. We need to approach it, organize, and execute properly.

LORA DENE KING. Another thing I wanted to tell you, when you said I'm doing this and that, I'm honored about that, but I'm going to tell you, you go through your valleys at your own time. I want to do a podcast. I haven't got there yet. It's like, we're both doing different things. I'm honored to have contact with you again and your soul, your energy. I love that. When you say "sis," I don't say that to people, so I appreciate that. And I appreciate you and I look forward to changing the world with our pain, with a smile, hold on to the strength of our fathers and who they were. You know, this is the right thing to do. This is the right thing to do to help. This is how I always felt. I can sit there and dwell in my emotions and spiral down, or I can change the world with that. I can help somebody else. I'm one situation away from being in this situation. I use my dad's strength. I ask, "How did he do that? How did he get up every day? Who am I not to do what I need to do?" So, I'm honored.

EMERALD GARNER. You don't understand how absolutely amazing that is. It's good to hear because sometimes you just need that pat on the back, you just need to hear "good job." You know what I'm saying? I'm glad that I created a space for us where we can call each other sisters in the movement, and when I say, "I've got you, sis," and you say, "I got you, sis," I believe you and you believe me.

LORA DENE KING. And we mean it and our intention is the same.

EMERALD GARNER. Our intention is absolutely the same.

LORA DENE KING. No seriously, and I will have a connection with you for life. I'm always here.

CHAPTER 11

Finding My Voice

Finding one's voice is often quite challenging. There are so many ways people find their voices. As I continued on my journey, I found many different ways to "speak." One of the modes of expression I found has been participating in a variety of panel discussions, at universities, churches, high schools, etc. I want to share some of these panels here.

A Discussion with Rev. Sharpton

EMERALD GARNER. Thank you so much for taking time to speak with me. Rev. Sharpton!

REV. SHARPTON. Thank you for inviting me! You are most welcome!

EMERALD GARNER. In my opinion when victims are thrown into activism, they don't really know what to do. They don't know which direction to take. In my case, I

95

didn't know where to start, where to go. In my case, I came to Huddle one day. I just started coming to the rallies on Saturdays, and that's where I learned the process. That's where I learned that this is how we get our stories out, how we organize marches, how we coordinate protesting and things of that nature.

REV. SHARPTON. Well I think that it is important for people to know, that you have remained loyal and have continued fighting for justice. Not only for yourself, you have been involved in a lot of other cases and other situations, which showed your sincerity. That you weren't just using the movement, you have become a leader in the movement. I think that you felt an obligation when what happened to your father happened, but I also felt that when your sister passed away, that she's depending on you. So we're proud of you and we recognize that in you!

EMERALD GARNER. Thank you so much. I appreciate it and I'm sure Erica is doing a happy dance up there in heaven. She's saying, "Go 'head, Emerald!" So let's jump right in. As I said, victims don't ask to be thrown into the fire. So my question is, how powerful is public pressure when someone is a victim of police brutality to get laws passed, to get policies in place?

REV. SHARPTON. I think that it's very powerful and necessary. Because if you don't create the climate, if you don't create the public outcry, then it is very difficult and nearly impossible to get the laws passed. Politicians react to public outcry because that's their voters. If their voters don't seem upset about it, they're not going to be pushed toward it. So you need both the legislators and you need the public. That's why the victims who suffered this are the ones you need out in front of it, because they need to be able to look you in the face and say, "No, I'm not gonna do nothing," and they can't do that and think they're gonna get our votes.

EMERALD GARNER. Mhmm. Absolutely right, we've been on the forefront and we've been all over the news all over everywhere, media news and everything, and I do feel like it had an effect, and I do feel that you know sometimes you just gotta get a little crazy. My little viral video with my finger and my bag, I truly feel like they really heard me, and I do feel like that had an impact on Pantaleo getting fired.

REV. SHARPTON. Absolutely! I think that had we not shown that kind of outrage, see it's one thing for civil rights leaders like me to say how a family is. It's another thing when you are in their face, and you are pointing and passionate, and they see the hurt and pain, and it goes viral. Because then they know that you do exist and we're not exaggerating, so you need all of that. I think that it is important because we're talking about real human beings, we're not talking about objects somewhere, so I think all of that is important. Otherwise, they would have let Pantaleo stay there.

EMERALD GARNER. Absolutely, I believe that as well. I've met with a couple of people who have been victims of police brutality. Sometimes they don't get, or sometimes they don't want, the media attention. They don't want their faces to be plastered all over because we get recognized everywhere as victims—oh, that's Eric Garner's daughter, or that's Sean Bell's wife, or that's Mike Brown's mother—so some victims don't want to be in the spotlight or be in the media. So what would you say to those victims who want to have a law like the Eric Garner law? What steps should they make to do that without media attention?

REV. SHARPTON. I think that they've got to be able to go and tell their stories directly to their legislators. And they have to deal with people that are in the media, and they've got to get their stories out. I think it's more effective if they're in the media because nobody can express the pain like they do, but there are times they may want to step back, then they need to make sure that the people they send know what they're doing and know how to do it and don't hurt the cause, but that they help the cause. Then there's a way of doing it, but it's better to have a collective strategy.

EMERALD GARNER. Absolutely, I agree. As you know, I took a step back after Erica passed away to make sure the children were straight, so you know I had National Action Network as my representative, so they did the right thing and so look where we are now, judicial hearing.

REV. SHARPTON. And you can go out front when you want, which you've done very well. There are times you need to take a day or so to yourself or be with the kids which you have to do. You always have to take care of your personal life and obligations and mental and spiritual health and physical health.

EMERALD GARNER. I know that sometimes there's a lot of groups, and I've seen it for myself that there's a lot of groups that come, and National Action is one of the groups that stayed when the cameras and the lights go away. I feel like there should be a collective, like we all can stand together. What kinds of things should we push for organizations to work together because we are stronger working together? You're here with this family, you're here with that family, but I want all the organizations to stand with us.

REV. SHARPTON. I think that the way to do that is for the families to say that these are the three things we want or four things we want. We want everybody involved, y'all may not work together but we want everybody involved. Y'all may not work together, but we want y'all to work together with us on this. When the families set the standard then I think they have no choice. But lemme tell you, I've been involved in the civil rights movement since I was twelve. There's always been division, there's always been different groups. You're never gonna get everybody together but you can get the majority if the family says, "This is where I want it, y'all can't disrespect each other on the movement for my family."

EMERALD GARNER. I agree because that's going to be my next push. Which is to get everybody together. I do feel that we are stronger together than when we're apart regardless of differences.

REV. SHARPTON. That's right.

EMERALD GARNER. Everybody has their own opinion, everybody has their own point of view. Everybody can be respected while still having different points of view.

REV. SHARPTON. That's right.

EMERALD GARNER. A lot of celebrities, they put up the hashtags and they send checks or some of them make a posting or do a private meeting. What can celebrities privately do aside from the meetings, aside from writing a check?

REV. SHARPTON. I think that celebrities can use their public platform. Whatever it is. You play a sport, do what LeBron did, "I can't breathe" right on the court. Do what some of the rappers do, go right into the studio, put Eric Garner's name into it, put Sean Bell's name into it. Use your platform as well as writing the check and doing the private meetings. Do it right then because you have people's attention. We don't expect celebrities to lead the marches, they don't have to do what I do or what other groups do. But in what you do, mix that in.

EMERALD GARNER. I absolutely agree! A lot of celebrities, they reach out to you and they say, "Hey, we just want to meet privately," but that's a way for them to step up and do something. That's awesome, that's great.

REV. SHARPTON. Yes!

EMERALD GARNER. Also, a lot of times I get, "Emerald, why do you protest, why do you march?" As you know, I was gonna get arrested if Pantaleo didn't get fired, and everybody was like, that's dumb, why would you do that? Can you explain the importance of protesting, marching, and civil disobedience?

REV. SHARPTON. Protests, marching, civil disobedience is to highlight a problem to be solved. You're not gonna solve a problem unless it is in people's face. What is Martin Luther King in history for? Martin Luther King was not a congressman, he was not a senator, he never held office. He raised the attention of the problem, that's why he went to jail. Everybody said, "Oh, Martin Luther King is in jail," that's why he marched. He used to say that there's two types of leaders—transactional, that's who makes deals, legislates, and transformative, that's the people that raise the attention. I think with you being there, sometimes with thousands, sometimes with just you and a couple of others. But it kept the focus on! If the focus isn't there, nobody's gonna respond. In order to make those in power respond, you gotta give them something to respond to.

EMERALD GARNER. Right.

REV. SHARPTON. And just your presence makes them have to respond.

EMERALD GARNER. That's a great way to put it! My last question for you, a question I added in at the last moment: If you could snap your fingers and make one thing happen to end police brutality or misconduct, what would that be?

REV. SHARPTON. My one thing would be that I would have a law that says: Police cannot choke and police can not use deadly force unless there is no other option, and they would have to prove that there was no other option. That would be my one thing.

EMERALD GARNER. Absolutely, and I agree. Thank you so much, Rev. Sharpton for doing this!

REV. SHARPTON. Proud of you! I've done TV all over the world, but now I'm big. I'm on the iPod of Emerald Garner. You can't get bigger than this!

EMERALD GARNER. Yes! Thank you!

A Conversation with Some Members of My Family

Although me and my family are sometimes at odds, we have constantly come together for the bigger purpose. Here we are in 2014 at the National Action Network headquarters speaking as a family. My brothers are at the beginning stages of finding their voices, but they are going to get there. I can see the desire, especially in Eric. We have all been thrust into this position of being forced into stepping out of our comfort zone. The following excerpt of this panel shows how important it is to have the right people in your corner who can support and help prepare you to step into the discovery of your voice but also assist you in your walk. Etan Thomas moderated the panel and did a great job as usual.

ETAN THOMAS. So, we want to definitely welcome you and thank you for coming out. First of all, Emerald, it's amazing to see you find your voice. You know when we first met was at the NBA All-Star Weekend in New York, and we were at Canaan Baptist Church. Two thousand five hundred Black and Brown young men attended—that was right after everything happened. I wanted Emerald to come and feel the support from the community. She didn't really want to talk.

I said, "Listen, you don't have to talk. Just come and you'll feel the support, and if you feel like talking, then just give me a little signal," and so she said a little bit and that was like the birth of everything. Then she started finding her voice. Talk about the process that you've gone through of finding your voice.

EMERALD GARNER. Like I said in the video [of my interview with Rev. Sharpton], the first march that we did was in DC, and I cochaired that march along with National Action Network. We got buses to come down to DC, and we did a big march. I rode back on the Huddle bus. That march took place on a Friday and Saturday, and then that following Monday. I started coming to Huddle, and I never stopped. I was coming every week. I would just say a little bit more each time, and it was like, "OK, I could do this. I could do a little chatting," but then they started to become overwhelming for me because it was repetitive. We weren't getting the justice we deserved. I got frustrated and then my sister passed away and then everything piled on top of me. I took my niece and my nephew. Now I'm a mom of three. It was just a lot going on. As Etan said when he invited me out to the event at the NBA All-Star Weekend, I was not talking. I was not speaking. I had to find my voice, I literally had to have people come to me and say, your voice is powerful. You need to speak more.

So, fast forward and Erica passes away, and Erica was the warrior, she was the one that was hitting the streets with the mega mic and she was doing it all. And I was like, "Erica, I can't. I just don't have the capacity to do all that." I took Alyssa when Erica was going out there. "OK, you go on, Erica, go out there. You wanna go on the bridge, go ahead. I got the kids, OK." And that's how it was. After Erica passed away, I just feel like her spirit came through me. That day when I was with my bag and my purse. I don't know where that came from. I was in the meeting. They didn't say what I wanted to hear. I asked him, "Are you prosecuting the cop or not?" And they told me no they were not. So I told them, "That's all I'm here for, and I don't really want to hear anything else because you're talking in the same circles that you were last time." So, I left, I went down the elevator, walked down the street and I'm like, "You know what, I'm sick of this, sick of all of this," and, well y'all saw it in the video. I was just like, I feel like that needed to happen. And thirty days later Pantaleo was fired.

ETAN THOMAS. They finally heard you?

EMERALD GARNER. Yes, they finally heard me.

ETAN THOMAS. Give her a round of applause, you know. I want to ask you this because I asked you before and since we just saw your interview with Rev. Sharpton, and Rev. Sharpton gets a lot of criticism, all the time in our community. But when speaking to the family members of the victims of police brutality, you all talk about him in such glowing terms, and express so much gratitude and thankfulness to him. And I see him helping. Especially when he's helping at a time when it seems like nobody else has helped, and I want y'all to talk about that part, and I do want to touch on that because he gets so much criticism all the time.

ESAW GARNER. You want me to take that?

ETAN THOMAS. Yes, please.

ESAW GARNER. Hello, everybody. Going back to the day that it happened, I was in shock. I didn't know what was what, I was just hearing so many stories of what happened and where is he and go here and go there, and I was just so confused. I sat in front of my building and I'm like, "I'm gonna wait for him to call me and tell me where to go. I'm gonna wait for him to call me," but that call never came through. I got a call from someone else that said they just put him in the ambulance and took him to the hospital. Meet him at the hospital. So, I'm like, "OK." My girlfriend was in the building, she jumped in the cab with me. I went to the hospital. Moving forward from there. I went home. I was destroyed. I didn't want to stay in my apartment. It was too many memories everywhere I looked. I just saw his face. I heard his voice. I felt his presence. After being married to somebody for twenty-three years and for them to go to work one morning and say, "Babe, I'll see you later," which is something you used to hearing every single day, but that particular day, he asked me for a kiss and out of all the years that we've been married, he never asked me for a kiss. He either took it or didn't get one. After everything happened, that Friday—he was killed on a Thursday—that Friday, I was crying, everybody was coming to the house giving their condolences and so on and so forth, and then Saturday morning I got a knock on the door. It was Rev. Sharpton. I have seen Rev. Sharpton on TV. Everything that I watch on TV, his name pops up all over the place, and I'm like looking through the peephole and I'm like, "Is that really Rev. Sharpton?" And he's like, "Yeah, Mrs. Garner, can you open the door?" Because I wasn't gonna open the door. I didn't know if I was being catfished. I didn't know what was going on. I'm looking out, and I opened the door and he's like, "I'm here in any capacity that you need me. Whatever it is that you need." I never had anybody come to me and tell me that they were gonna give me whatever I wanted, whatever I needed, just to make sure that I'm stress-free. That's what he's been to me. I used to say "daddy dad," but then I found out that we were too close in age. So, then I said, "OK, you gotta be my big brother." Now he calls me his little sister and we have our own relationship. I can call him in the middle of the night. He'll answer his phone. I can call him at 4:30 in the morning when he's working out, having his fruit bowls and his hot tea, running on the treadmill, I can call him in the middle of his TV show, he might not answer me then but as soon as he get off that TV show, he's gonna call me and say, "Esaw, what happened?" You know? And it's like he's been there for me and he's still there for me five years later. There is nothing in this world that I have asked for or needed or wanted or anything that Rev. Sharpton wasn't there 100 percent. If he couldn't be there physically, he sends somebody in his place. If he can't send somebody in his place, "Esaw, can you possibly make it another day and I promise, I'll be there." Everybody tried to say, "You know when you get your money, you gonna have to pay him back," and I say, "You know what, people go by what they hear and not what they know, OK." I know for a fact and people should know too. He got TV shows. He got radio shows. You hear Rev. Al Sharpton all over the place. Even as I was watching *Everybody Hates Chris* and something happened and he said, "Well maybe I should have called Al Sharpton," you know what I'm saying? That man got more money than the law allows. He don't need my money. He don't need no victim's money. He paid the damn taxes. If he didn't they would've came and got him a long time ago. So, it bothers me too when people talk what they don't know. It bothers me. I go on the Internet, and I answer and I comment sometimes.

EMERALD GARNER. She claps back y'all.

ESAW GARNER. Y'all, yeah! I clap back all the time for Rev. And even with his daughters. I'd be like, "Dominique, did you hear what they said about Rev. Sharpton?" She'd say, "Esaw, don't worry about it, we're used to it. Don't let it bother you." And I'm like, "I can't because I'm not the type to bite my tongue, so it's hard for me to just sit back and say nothing." Emerald is finding her voice, I have no problem expressing how I feel. Now, if I do it the best way, that's another thing. [*Laughter from the crowd.*] Me and the media don't get along because they said some things that didn't come out of my mouth and twisted it around and made it sound completely different. It's like texting somebody something and them taking it in but not the way you meant it. Taking your words out of context, you know what I'm saying? So, I fell back about two years ago. I stopped doing interviews. I stopped going places and doing things because me, I just want to do grandma things. I want to go spend time with the grandkids. That's my happiness. It's time for the young people to take up this fight for justice. That's why I am so proud of Emerald and of everything Erica did, and I'm excited to see whoever else wants to start using their voice, but no pressure if they just want to live their lives because that is definitely their right. But with that being said, Etan, a lot of people have misconceptions about Rev. Sharpton.

ETAN THOMAS. Right.

ESAW GARNER. And I've seen nothing but good. I've had people stop me on the street and try to tell me things that he's done years ago, and I just look at them and say, "Girl, bye." All I say is, "If that's the way you feel, you are entitled to your opinion, but don't try to project your opinion on me. Don't try to make me change how I feel about Rev. Sharpton." And like I tell everybody, I don't do interviews and stuff, but if the Rev. called me and said, "Esaw, I need you to come with me to do MSNBC," I'm there. Arthritis, in pain, pain pills in my pocket. Whatever, I'm there, whatever he needs me to do, whatever he asks me to do, I always do. And I've seen first-hand how he has helped my daughters find their voice. He encouraged them when they were at their lowest and supported them when not many other people were.

ETAN THOMAS. And I'm glad you said that and made that clear for people because, like you said, people have a lot of misconceptions and things that they hear and they just repeat it. And it spreads like rapid fire, they have no facts. You speak right to the source and hear from them, as far as their dealings with Rev. Sharpton.

Now, Eric, you're finding your voice as well. I heard you tell a story. We were on the *Karen Hunter Show*, it's a story that I haven't really heard, and we have a lot of guys that are athletes in the audience and they would really relate to that story you told. Tell the story that you told on air about where you were when you heard and how your teammates responded to you and that whole process, because I never heard you tell that story before.

ERIC GARNER JR. Sure, how's everybody doing? All right, I was at a championship basketball game when I got the news. Well, I didn't get the news till I got in the house, but everybody that was on the bus with me on the way back already heard. My phone was in my bag. I didn't pull it out. We just won the championship. We were on our way back and everybody was just looking at me funny. They were being real uncomfortable acting you know. Some guys gave me a hug but it wasn't like a celebratory hug because we had just won the championship, it was like a consoling hug. But I didn't understand why. I didn't know what to expect until I got home.

ETAN THOMAS. And then what happened after that?

ERIC GARNER JR. My moms told me, and then I had to attend college. I was going to college on a scholarship. Like two weeks later. I had to go to school and I just stayed in my room for the rest of the two weeks that I was home then I went to school. That was it.

ESAW GARNER. I remember Eric came home and he said, "Mom, call Daddy." I said, "Call him for what? I just spoke to him. He said he's coming in early. I'm not going to bother him. Let him do what he do. I'll see him later." He said, "Nah, Ma, I just heard that he got choked out on Bay Street," and I'm like, "Huh," and that's when my phone started ringing. I had two phones at the time, and both phones were just ringing, ringing, ringing, ringing. I didn't know what was going on. I just came in the house. I was watching TV, relaxing, and he walked outside and he was like, "My poor daddy!" You know because I just heard that the cops choked daddy out on Bay Street, and I was like, "Huh?" you know. And that was at a quarter to three. I can't forget the time because I was watching *People's Court*, one of my favorite shows. I had just talked to him at like about 2:30, something like that, had just spoken to him, and he was telling me, I'm coming in early because the cops are rolling around and they're messing with me. So, I'm coming in. I said, "Eric, just come in the house, call it an early day." Three o'clock is when I got the phone call to go to the hospital and that he was at the hospital. To this day, I haven't seen past the first three minutes of the video. I can't watch it, you know. I don't know. People have come to me and told me you know his eyes rolled back. He went limp. He was already gone before they put him in the ambulance, but I didn't see it for myself. But just to hear it and knowing what kind of person he was? He didn't deserve that on any level. Regardless, I know people that shot police, shot with police, fight with police, throw things at police, and they still walking around to tell about. My husband was a boxer, a good one. If he wanted to resist arrest, he could have punched a couple of them cops out. I swear, I know my husband. If he would have known that, that was his last breath that he was taking, he would have gone all out. He would not have stood there and let them do what they did. He would have just fought, but he had no idea that that was going to be his last words and his last breath, you know. So, excuse me y'all. [*Begins to cry.*]

ETAN THOMAS. That's all right, that's all right. Talking about it, the way that you have your strength, and this is one thing that I've expressed to Emerald. Her strength has been inspirational for other people. [*Applause.*] When Alton Sterling's son in particular was really inspired by your words, your strength and your courage. Talk about this as difficult as it is. You took it on and continue doing as you've seen the inspiration happen and how it's been therapeutic for you. I want you to really touch on that because the therapy part is a part that in our community, we don't really utilize therapy the way that we should. We have all types of trauma going on, and we don't really do therapy just as a whole. Talk about that, how much that has benefited you to speak about it and the inspiration that you've had for other people, and the fact that you wouldn't have been able to find your voice without taking care of your mental health.

EMERALD GARNER. Well, going back to Alton Sterling's son. He has an older son. I think he was about thirteen or fourteen at the time. I went to an event and I met him and this was after I learned to speak a little bit. I went to Franklin K. Lane [High School] that week to go speak, after that we met again at the NAN Huddle. Next time was another event where I met him. He said, "I feel so passionate to speak because," he said, "I'm the oldest of all my father's kids." I have a lot of young kids after me, it's inspiring for me to see another victim who's a child. I'm not calling you a kid but another child of the movement pretty much. Like, in Shawn Belle's situation, his daughters were young. In Mike Brown's situation. He did not have kids. Amadou Diallo, I don't think he had any children either.

ETAN THOMAS. Right.

EMERALD GARNER. A lot of people forget about the kids. Just the other day, me and my brothers were sitting there and the lady was like, "Are you guys relatives of Eric Garner?"

I said, "We are his children." People often forget that Eric Garner was a grown man with a wife and children. Alton Sterling's son brought me back to that. I thought, "Oh, right, we do have a voice." A lot of people like to speak for us, and he was the one that turned me on to that. It clicked for me. I have a voice too! What I say matters! Who's better to represent Eric Garner than his children? We are a combination of Eric and Esaw. He created us. He raised us. I have twenty-two years of memories of my father. Not two, not three. He was never an absentee father. He was never not there. I don't know what it is to be a fatherless child. I don't know what that means. He brought me back to reality because I was just so spaced out. I was at a point in my life where I was spaced out, and when Etan talked about the therapy part, Etan knows, I text him all the time. I'm very impulsive. I'm very angry. I'm very aggressive, and I snap at the drop of a dime. I really do, and I'm the type of person, I don't think first, I act first. So, I try to think like an adult. I tell Etan, "I'm gonna grow up one day, might not be today, but I'm gonna grow up one day."

ESAW GARNER: Your mother didn't grow up yet. [*Audience laughs.*] But that's why, and I know I keep repeating myself, but that's why I am so proud that you have found your voice and your ability to articulate your passion in a way that it can be heard. Y'all are your father's children. So he lives through you all now. You, Eric, Emery, even the babies. Your father lives through all of you.

◊ ◊ ◊

That really stuck with me. The panel went on and on for another hour and a half, and we covered a lot. It was emotional at times, I don't think there was a dry eye on the panel. Everyone shed some tears quite a few times, but my mother was absolutely right. We were all finding our way. My brother Emery is finding his way the best he can. Eric is finding his way, and his way may look different from my way, and that's OK because at the end of the day, we all love each other, and we are all still grieving no matter how many years have passed by. Even though my oldest sister, Shardinee, did not choose to speak on the panel, she came to give her support. We're all still dealing with the patriarch of our family being taken away from us, and we all are taking different journeys to continue through life. But my journey has led me to be ready to carry the mantle of this fight. I will always dedicate myself to fighting for my father's memory and changing the world in his name. I am the daughter of Eric Garner, and I wear that title with pride.

A Panel with Angel McCoughtry, Renee Montgomery, Tierra Ruffin-Pratt, and Elizabeth Williams of the WNBA

I have always admired the WNBA, but after I saw how they all banded together to stand up for the families of survivors and fight for justice for the victims of police brutality, I was blown away. I wished I could give each and every one of them a hug and just thank them all personally. I mean, going back to the back-to-back murders of Philando Castile and Alton Sterling in 2016, the way the entire WNBA banded together was amazing. And at first, their president made a public statement that if any of them wear a BlackLivesMatter T-shirt as their warm-ups or protests in any way, shape, or form, they will be fined and suspended. But they all did it together, so they couldn't suspend everyone because they would have nobody to play games.

It was such an honor to be included on a panel with two Atlanta Dream players: Renee Montgomery (who took a year off from playing in the WNBA to focus on activism after the murders of George Floyd and Breonna Taylor) and Elizabeth Williams (who is currently the longest-tenured member of the Dream). Montgomery and Williams discussed what prompted their revolt against their team owner Kelly Loeffler and detailed how the team banded together (along with the help of the entire WNBA) to elect Loeffler's opponent, Warnock, who was polling at a lowly 9 percent before the Atlanta Dream and the WNBA got involved.

They support each other. They made sure that they were all informed. Even the players who weren't from the United States were brought up to speed, and they jumped right on board and showed support because they felt their teammates' pain. Now, those efforts did not only cause Kelly Loeffler to lose her Senate race but also played a role in her selling the team. That's just amazing to me, and they possess the type of unity and collaborative work that I want to create for the survivors. They are the perfect model of that.

The WNBA players have already etched their names in the history books for athlete activism, and now they are adding additional chapters of accomplishments. They deserve all the praise and accolades for their bravery and courage.

ETAN THOMAS. Welcome to this Martin Luther King Jr. edition of *The Rematch*. We are here with some great WNBA players. Emerald Garner, Eric Garner's daughter, is here. We

have Elizabeth Williams. We have Angel McCoughtry and
Tierra Ruffin-Pratt, and we also have Renee Montgomery.
I'm really looking forward to this discussion. We're celebrating Dr. Martin Luther King Jr.'s birthday this weekend and
the spirit of activism that is alive and kicking right now. A
lot of times when we talk about Martin Luther King, we talk
about him as if everything that he fought for, everything that
he struggled for, is all over and everything is just fine now.
And as we saw just a week or two ago, right here at the US
Capitol, the struggle is far from over. I wanted to talk about
everything in terms of the work and the activism that the
WNBA has been doing in particular. I followed all of y'all
for a very long time, and I'm a big fan. First of all, talk about
the correlation between everything that Martin Luther King
Jr. stood for—injustice anywhere is a threat to justice everywhere. Talk about that in terms of how it is relative today. I
want to start with Angel. You have been active in this for a
long time this past season, you were the main one responsible
for the "Black Lives Matter" and the "Say Her Name" that
was worn on the jerseys and everything. Talk about how and
why that was important and how that relates to everything
that Dr. King fought for his entire life.

ANGEL MCCOUGHTRY. I would say, we just want to
continue to keep the legacy alive and fight. John Lewis said,
"It's always OK to get in some good trouble," you know,
and we just wanted to make a statement. How the idea came
about was really, I just wanted to figure out a way how can
we use our platforms to continue to fight for social justice
and continue to show everybody that we care even while
we're playing. We're not just playing and ignoring everything that's going on out there. So, that's kind of how that

idea came about and everybody responded well to it. All the girls participated and wore it, and just that togetherness I have never seen. So, together, and that's when I realized, "Wow, there's power in numbers!" I think that relates to Martin Luther King, us standing together. We're one nation, and I always tell this story to people. I was in France one time, and somebody was like, "Why do you guys always refer to Black and white? Aren't you all American?" That always stuck with me, because I feel like, as a country why do we divide so much? In being one country that should be together, and we're dividing everything up in one country. That always stuck with me, and as Martin Luther King said, he had that dream that we will all be together as one. I still believe in that dream. I don't think that dream has faded out. It just takes a lot of time.

ETAN THOMAS. That's a good point, and, Tierra, I want to talk about the organizing. Along the same lines of what Angel was talking about when you were playing for the Mystics, that's where I really saw you. After the back-to-back murders of Philando Castile and Alton Sterling and the organizing that you did with the Mystics and helping with the media blackout and everything that the Mystics did as a whole. Can you talk about that in particular, and, also, a two-part question: How did y'all get everybody involved? I've asked you that before because you know that is something. That's very unique because, y'all meant everybody. It was Black players, white players, foreign players, players they ain't even from here, don't even know really what's going on but y'all got them all involved and all their support. Talk about how you did that?

TIERRA RUFFIN-PRATT. For me, because I had already experienced a death of a family member by the hands of the police, I had a really strong attachment to everything that was going on. Especially with all the killings that was happening at that time, and I think my teammates just kind of backed me when I was like, I think we should do a blackout. This should be a time where we stand together as one team and just only focus on what's going on right now in this country, and my teammates were like, "OK!" My coaches were like, "OK!" I think that with them having my back, it gave me the extra push to just keep going with everything I wanted to do after that, but my teammates, the coaches, everybody just said, "Yeah! We need to speak up, use our platform," and that was the beginning, with us doing it. Minnesota did it, and all the other teams kind of like trickled down and followed, but the league has always been at the forefront of things like with everything that's going on in the world. The WNBA has kind of been one of those leagues that speaks out. We don't really have any fear of what will happen to us. So, we just kind of speak what we think is necessary, and everybody else kind of followed. I think if some of the players are like, "No, we're not going to do it." They would have been looked at a little bit different, and I think everybody was kind of on board. In fact, like we see all the negative stuff and all the bad things that are going on in this country. Nobody's speaking out. So, why not use our platform and do something that's right and that kind of made it all easier because we were all on one accord.

ETAN THOMAS. I think it's just amazing because when Kaepernick first took his knee, he was kind of out there by himself. But with y'all, everybody did it together, and I just really commend y'all for that. Elizabeth, this a few weeks ago, we saw what y'all did. With really changing Georgia into a blue state. I mean I never would have really thought that Georgia would have flipped blue honestly, and the way that you all also formed and banded together and really are responsible for Loeffler not winning. Also at the same time, she was, and I don't use the word *owner* for obvious reasons, but she was one of the CEOs of your team, and you were all banning against her. I just thought that that is amazing. It is something I don't feel like there's enough praise for, all the work that all of y'all have done, that the WNBA has done. And that's why I really want to use the platform that I have and I'm thankful for BasketballNews.com for featuring this and FLYTV. How did that come about and did you receive any resistance? Walk me through the whole process.

ELIZABETH WILLIAMS. Yeah, it was interesting because when she made those statements, it was right as we had gotten into the bubble. We were still in our quarantine period. Some people weren't with us. Our team along with the staff, we had a Zoom call because we're like, "Hey, we have to address this. We have to at least say something."

ETAN THOMAS. No wait, wait a second. Say the exact statements, because she talked about when everyone was talking about George Floyd and Breonna Taylor and the exact statements that she said was something to the effect of, you know, she called everybody the mob. Say the exact same thing.

ELIZABETH WILLIAMS. Like this bottom mentality saying "Black lives matter" is Marxist and to keep politics out of sports and to wear the American flag on our jersey and all this stuff that ironically was about putting politics into sports. That alone was very ironic, but for us, our team, we wanted to make a statement, but we also wanted to have an action behind it. We didn't really know what that was going to look like, and other players throughout the week had supported us, said, "Hey, we're with you guys, whatever you want to do." As we were brainstorming ideas, we realized we couldn't really do anything about her ownership. That's on the league, but she is in the Senate seat, and we can do something about that. And we had connections with Lisa Borders, who was our former president, and she's heavy into politics, and Stacey Abrams on our union's board of advocates. So, at least we had connections with people who understood politics, and they were able to connect us with Rev. Warnock. After vetting him, having conversations with him, we said, "We can have a call that's open to every player who wants to hear who this guy is." Ultimately, we decided. We're going to support him. We knew it was going to be even more powerful. Having the entire league backing us. So when we were in Atlanta and had our first nationally televised game, we wore these "Vote Warnock" shirts along with every other team in the league, and it was this incredible movement! Ultimately Warnock ended up winning the runoff in January.

ETAN THOMAS. You all mobilized to really cause her to lose in this race. I want to say that because at the beginning Warnock was polling at 9 percent.

RENEE MONTGOMERY. Yeah.

ETAN THOMAS. That's where he was polling.

RENEE MONTGOMERY. Yeah.

ETAN THOMAS. People have to always remember that there was a big change after the whole WNBA got around and campaigned around him, pushing him to get that spot. I want you to talk about how that came about and how he was able to mobilize in that way, because it's something monumental. We don't see anything like this, and it hasn't been given attention. I feel that it should have been because we haven't seen this level of mobilization in the NBA, NFL, MLB, NHL, no other organization and you all did it. Just walk me through first of all, how did that come about? How did you do that?

RENEE MONTGOMERY. Yeah, you have to give it up to the social justice council and the WNBA, the executive committee, because these are groups of women that organized. It wasn't just actions all over the place in chaos. This was a very organized movement, and they vetted Raphael Warnock, Senator Warnock. They wanted to see who he was and what they brought to the council. They brought in advisers to help them because this isn't necessarily the space that we're used to roaming, so all that was done. Then I got a text from Sue Bird saying, hey, I just wanted to let you know what's going on from inside the bubble. We're creating these shirts that say, "Vote Warnock." This is what we've done. She broke it all down for me. She was like, "You know I wanted you to know because you're boots on the ground here in Atlanta," and I'm like, "What, this is crazy! This is lit in a sense." It was... I love when things are planned, you know? This is not a vindictive movement. This is a "we're trying to get somewhere" movement, and this is who can get us there and so it was exciting just to see how everyone was banding together.

ETAN THOMAS. I think it was really amazing. The way that you all organized. In my previous book, *We Matter: Athletes and Activism*, I asked Swin Cash, How you all do that? You know what I mean? Like, how did y'all do that? And her response was simply, "Well, women do things differently." She was like, "We support each other, and it could be somebody we know and love." That was her honest answer. She's like, "That's all I can really tell you." What all of y'all are telling me in common is that there really wasn't a lot of coaxing or trying to convince anyone. Y'all made a call and everybody was like, "OK, I'm with it," and then y'all did it. It was as simple as that.

ANGEL MCCOUGHTRY. Well, Etan, let me add to that real quick. We did do our research. We didn't want to say "OK!" We're not just going to put on "Vote Warnock" shirts because Kelly made these statements. We did our research about health care. Let's compare the two. Let's compare the two about the LGBTQ community. Let's compare the two about social injustice, and besides the words that she said, of course what we didn't agree with. We did the research and we did see that Warnock was more for the people and for our vote, after doing the research and of course they put it together. It worked out.

ELIZABETH WILLIAMS. Yeah, it was perfect because not only were we supporting this guy, but he supports all the things we've been talking about, like criminal justice reform.

ANGEL MCCOUGHTRY. Yeah.

ELIZABETH WILLIAMS. Women's health, you know. We're a league of Black women. All these things that we're talking about, it's the perfect opportunity. We've been talking about voting. So now we can promote someone and vote for someone who essentially can legislate and put in policies that are beneficial for us in the long run.

ETAN THOMAS. Well, Emerald. I want to ask you something, Emerald, because we've been doing a lot of work together for a while. It's interesting that a lot of times you hear some of the older generation say, what is activism? They criticize the current age of activists and of athletes comparing them to the athletes of the past like Muhammad Ali and they say, "OK, well, activism has died." I had a big debate with Bill Rhoden, whose book is great. It's called *Forty Million Dollar Slaves*. We just disagree on a lot of different portions of it. One of the things he asked was, is wearing a T-shirt really activism, and he always says that. "Is it really activism? Is it the same thing?" And I always say, "Well! If you talk to a family member of a victim of police brutality, they can tell you what seeing athletes wear those T-shirts and wearing and having that support means." So, I wanted to ask you, Emerald, what does that mean, to see an entire league supporting your father? Seeing an entire league risking everything with their job to stand up and say, "OK, no, this isn't right and we need to change." What does that mean to you?

EMERALD GARNER. It means everything. It means that my father's name is gonna live on. Means that you know us. Victims are not being ignored because nine times out of ten, well really the majority of the time, when you see activists, they kind of haven't been through what we've been through as victims. Now I say I'm a survivor, but I was a victim at one point, and when I say *victim* I absolutely mean my father was taken away from me in the worst possible way on television, and the fact that I see WNBA players and I see NBA players, and I see other athletes standing up for social justice, it's like, "OK, so, you have this big platform. We have things going on in neighborhoods that you guys are from." Of course nobody is born with a silver spoon in their hand unless their last name is Abercrombie and Fitch or something like that. We're at the level where we're thrust into the social justice movement. It's a situation where we learn about social justice. We learn about Martin Luther King, we learn about Sojourner Truth, we learn about Rosa Parks in school, but then you hit the real world. Nobody can prepare you for your father or your loved one being killed on national television and having to live with that for the rest of your life. People not knowing that I am my father's child and they're sitting there talking about the situation without being mindful of what they're saying. To see that I have that support, as you say, it's the support, the support is everything. I always say my sister did not survive the movement. She died of a massive heart attack at twenty-seven with no prior health histories besides mild asthma, mild bronchitis, like my sister has never had to use the asthma pump. She's always been an athlete. She played basketball. She followed WNBA. She was the basketball guru of the family. We had the boys, but then there was Erica. Then when she took that energy and put it into activism. It was just so much, so much, so much, so much, and she wasn't getting the support. She was out Tuesdays and Thursdays. For two years protesting with less than ten people, then you have the Tamika Mallorys and you have the other activists. I'm not saying that they're doing something wrong, but they haven't been through what we've been through. So to see that they get more support than the family member, for me it was a slap in the face. I was twenty-two when my father passed away. I had a whole twenty-two years with my father, he's never been absent, never been a deadbeat. I could always call my father for something, and now it's like my sole provider is not here and I have to watch him be killed on the TV continuously and then every time something happens, his name is being brought up. When George Floyd was murdered, it felt like I was back in 2014 because now the media wants to talk and ask how do you feel? You know how I feel because I've been screaming in front of the monument and in front of the memorial site. I've been screaming in front of the courthouse, you know exactly how I feel.

ETAN THOMAS. And you know Emerald, you see her, you see the passion. We've done a lot of events together, and you hear the passion in her voice and then you hear the pain in her voice and it hurts me to hear the pain. When she talks about what she had to go through and it's just so frustrating. When you hear people criticize and you just say OK. Right now, we're celebrating Martin Luther King's holiday, this weekend and so whenever anybody protests in any kind of way, the main thing that a lot of the opposition says is, "Well you should do it like Martin Luther King did it." Ms. Renee Montgomery, how are you doing?

RENEE MONTGOMERY. I'm doing good!

ETAN THOMAS. Listen, I appreciate you coming on and talking to me! There's a lot that I want to talk to you about. You did something, and you were following in the footsteps of your old teammate Maya Moore. You stepped away from the game in order to be able to focus on social justice. I want you to walk me through the decision to do that and what led up to it.

RENEE MONTGOMERY. Oh yeah, you know, the civil unrest is pretty much what led up to it. Just everything going on in America. I had a second. I was still for a moment. When you're still, you have time to think about things, see what's going on, and to make a long story short, just like everyone else, I didn't like what I was seeing. I didn't like seeing George Floyd murdered. I didn't like what happened to Ahmaud Arbrey or Breonna Taylor. There were so many things that I'm like, "Man!" We already knew what was going on, but when you're still and you're looking at it, you have to just sit with it, and it didn't sit right with me, and that's pretty much what led to my decision. I just wanted to have boots on the ground. I wanted to be here in Atlanta to see what changes and what positive effect I could have on the community here, and, man, it turned into something bigger. It just started from just me watching the news and just not, not feeling it.

ETAN THOMAS. Right. Let's go back a little bit. How do you respond to some of the criticism that you all received? I want to go one by one because I'm sure you've received a lot of backlash, a lot of criticism. And that's a testament to your strength because you kept going, but let's start with Angel. Talk about the criticism that you received when you all made your statement. When you all put everything on display. Don't say her name, just the criticism. As far as, let's keep that out of sports. You just focus on basketball. Just talk about the criticism you received.

ANGEL MCCOUGHTRY. Yeah, I had a couple of bad messages. People calling me the n-word in my DMs and stuff like that, but with Emerald, her passion, if they could just see that and hear that. I really wish Kelly was on this call right now. You know I played for Atlanta for ten years. So, I really got to know Kelly as well. She needs to hear stuff like this because they really don't understand or get it. They hang in that social circle and then when you get to a certain financial status, everything's easy. You kind of lose that touch of reality. This is where these people need to hear that stuff because they don't get it or they wouldn't denounce "Black lives matter" as if it's just nothing. They wouldn't get mad when we say it. We never said "Black lives matter means we're better than you," because we never have been, we've said we want to be equal. So, as far as criticism, I couldn't care less because we march peacefully, you kill Martin Luther King, you know. You complain, you kill Medgar Evers. These people have done nothing to anyone. They were peaceful, you know. You, you create these stereotypes and you kill innocent people through the cops. What do we care about criticism at this point? Then you get mad that we protest and yell and scream. Criticism at this point means nothing. We're demanding change and, Emerald, thank you for what you've been doing. We're going to get our change. We will fight to the end and criticism means nothing at this point, honestly.

ETAN THOMAS. That's right. That's great, Tierra, the same question to you about the criticism that you received after, because honestly I want you to talk about this part as well. You all kind of forced the WNBA to go along with what you all were doing because at first they said they were going to fine everybody, and they said, don't do that. When, I believe, it was the Minnesota Lynx after that when the policeman walked off their posts and everybody in the WNBA panicked like, "Oh, OK, oh Lord! We're making the police mad. Nobody do that again." Then that empowered y'all and the whole league, did it? I keep emphasizing that point, because I thought that was so dope because we've never seen anything like that in any league at any time where everybody got together the same way. Talk about how you all withstood the criticism?

TIERRA RUFFIN-PRATT. I, I just don't think we care like Angel said. It doesn't matter right now. We're fighting for something way bigger than just us. I think as a league, we see that, and we know that, and we know that we're going to get criticism. We get criticized just playing basketball itself. So, of course if we're fighting for something that not a lot of people want to hear, we're going to get criticized for it. But we get criticized for doing our job every day. So, if we're fighting for something greater than that. I don't think it really matters. As a league with Black women and Black players and Black coaches, I think we just get to a point where you're like, I really don't hear the outside noise because I know what I'm doing is far greater than what they're saying about me or about us as a league. It's always going to be some people that don't agree with what you're doing. If you let those people stop, you won't get anywhere. I think we just got to a point where it's like, I'm tired of not saying anything, they always tell athletes, "Uh, keep politics out of the sport," "Uh, shut up and dribble," all of that type stuff but at what point are we just citizens, what point are we just human, at what point? We're not just basketball players, we're not just athletes, we're people. So, we're going to fight for the people not just because we're athletes, we're fighting because we're Black in America or we see that Blacks in America are being done wrong. Until you get to a point where criticism doesn't bother you, you'll never be able to prosper and you'll never be able to create the change that's needed in this world. I think we've gotten to that point where the criticism is just whispers and goes in through one end and out through one end of the other.

ETAN THOMAS. Those are great points! Elizabeth, you know y'all are in Georgia, I like it. If people didn't know, I played a year with the Hawks, and I know like there's certain parts of Atlanta that is like popping and it's great there's a whole lot of us. Then you go to some of them other parts, and you're like, Oh Lord! Did I go back in time like a few decades, you know? So, talk about the level of criticism that y'all must have received in Georgia while you were pushing for the Senate to flip in something that, I don't know, has that ever happened before? Something this monumental! In this day and age.

ELIZABETH WILLIAMS. Yeah, I mean it's really what Angel and T said. We don't really care. We've had critics since we started being female professional athletes. So, it's never been about us individually. It's been about this bigger movement, it's been about finding unique ways this year to help. It looked like supporting Rev. Warnock in 2016, it was DC and Minnesota wearing the shirts and protesting early. So, we found really different ways to support and promote these social justice movements. That's not going to change regardless of the critics. Even being in Georgia, I guess there were a little bit more critics with what was going on, but you're also fueled by the positive messages that you receive. I think always because the world can sometimes seem so heavy, it's nice to have people behind you that say, "You guys are doing the right thing," you know. "We support you." "We hear you." I feel that those messages for me carry a lot more weight than any of the negativity that I see, and we're reminded that we're on the right side of history.

ETAN THOMAS. You know one of the things that we've done. I'm blessed to have three beautiful kids. Me and my wife watched *Selma* around this time. We were watching *Selma* with our kids last year, and there was the part where my daughter Imani asked, "Were all white people against us?" You're watching a movie, and that's how it looks. I said, "All right, well just hold on, just hold on, just wait," and she was like, "All right but this don't look good. I mean, just like no white people were on our side." So, then it got to the part where right before they were about to cross Edmund Pettus Bridge, and all the white clergy from all across the country stood with them, and they saw the police not attack them now. The scene like a little bit before that, if you remember, at night, and it was just them protesting and the police came and it was violent. They were violently attacking all of the peaceful protesters so much. So, I had to pause it and be like, "All right? You all right, Imani, like everything cool?" She's like, "Yeah, I'm all right but it was really intense." So, now she saw where all the white clergy stood with them and she saw the police pause, and she's like, "Wow!" She's like, "So, they only paused because the white people was with us," and then she said, "Well, it was great to see that some white people stood with us." And then she said, "So, that's why we need more white people to stand with us on this." And she just boom boom boom made the connections, and I wanted to ask y'all about that. How important is it to have white allies? To have your white teammates stand with you because there's some things where there's a certain demographic. Certain demographic formations of America that's only going to hear it from a white voice. That's just the way that it is, that's the honest truth. You can have LeBron, you can have Steph Curry, you can have anybody say it, but they only gonna hear it if Popovich says it or Steve Kerr says it. That is the honest truth. Talk about how important it is to have your white teammates in particular stand with you. Angel! You can go first.

ANGEL MCCOUGHTRY. Yeah, it is so important because I think our Caucasian teammates realize, we all have a story, we don't really have a story. We all have some kind of mistreatment or misconduct toward us, you know. So, I think they get it. They've learned our culture. They've learned who we are. They embrace us. They think we're cool, they love our music. They love how we cook. They get us. They understand us, and I think they want to make it a point to show the world. Hey! You're misunderstanding who you think they are. I'm around them every day. They're me. I am them. I just think that and I'm so proud of the girls who have stood up. And the men and all sports, the Caucasians who have stood up for us, because we need their voices because sometimes when we keep crying and keep crying, people like, "Oh, here they go again."

ETAN THOMAS. Right.

ANGEL MCCOUGHTRY. But when they see that, no this is true, they are right. Then it can be taken a little more seriously and they realize that too. So, it helps.

ETAN THOMAS. Definitely you agree with me. Tierra, same question.

TIERRA RUFFIN- PRATT. Oh, all right. I think they have a hard time trying to understand, but once they understand what we've gone through, or what we're going through, they're more accepting and more understanding and more willing to speak up. A lot of them don't know how, because I've been asked, whether it's by my teammates in the league or kids I train or just people I'm around, white people that I'm around, "How can we help, or what can we do?" I think when those questions are starting to be asked, we're moving in the right direction, because before they would just let stuff happen and watch us try to do what we can and just sit back even when they see things are wrong and they would sit back and not say anything. But now, I think it's gotten to a point where I've had teammates sit in meetings and cry. White teammates sit in meetings and cry because they're like, "I don't understand how we haven't spoken up before now. I don't understand why we haven't taken that step already." I think now they're more open to speaking out. They're not afraid just like we aren't afraid anymore. They aren't afraid because for them it's family heritage. It's generations before them that they're afraid of. It's the people in their families that were raised differently and have a different mental and different mindset than them. So, I think now it's like, "Well, like us you just gotta speak up. Like it's time to just speak up and say something, and if we speak up and speak out, we know that we're helping those who are around every day and we see them as people, not Black people, not just athletes, not just basketball players, but friends, teammates, family." I think it gets to a point where it's like, "If we're not speaking up for our family, we're not doing the right thing, and we don't want to be on that side."

ETAN THOMAS. Very well said, very well said. Elizabeth, same question.

ELIZABETH WILLIAMS. Yeah, I think one thing a lot of our white friends and white teammates have realized is, we're past, "Oh, I didn't know, oh, I don't know." We're in the age where there is information everywhere. If you want to know something, you can find out if you like. If you have a true, a real deep conversation with your Black teammates, you will learn something that you didn't know before. I do think similar to what Tierra said, they're not afraid anymore. They've had these conversations with us. They've taken in what is true. They realize that the history that we're taught in schools is very limiting. They've also, in doing that, they've understood that their voice carries a different weight than ours, and so that's how I think a lot of them feel. We've seen the white allyship in our league, and it's helped us be really successful. It's not just the voices that you're hearing. It's the white voices as well. I think they're understanding that they can't sit on ignorance anymore. That's what's helping us move forward for sure.

ETAN THOMAS. Right, right. And, Emerald, I want you to talk. It's so amazing because people don't understand that when I first met Emerald, she didn't say anything, she was quiet and couldn't really talk. Couldn't really express everything to you because she was still dealing with the trauma of everything. She's grown into this big confident voice, and the way she's using her platform and taking on the mantle of fighting for justice, for her father but also changing the laws so that it doesn't keep happening to the next person behind her, the next person. And you're working on a book. I'm so proud of you, Emerald. And everything that you're doing. I just want you to talk a little bit about your book that you're working on, you know just how you developed your voice. That's what I want you to talk about real quick: how you developed your voice to be able to speak out on everything.

EMERALD GARNER. Well, coming out and talking about my father at first, I would just attend the press conference and everything. I would say everything I needed to say behind closed doors, and when I would talk to my friends, people would ask, "Why don't you just say that when you have the chance to talk, why don't you say that?" I'm like, "You know, it was a power struggle for who's going to be in the spotlight, who's going to talk." Everybody in my family was older, and everybody was looking at my father's mother. So when I got invited to the NBA All-Star panel discussion that Etan put together in Harlem, I was living in Harlem, and he reached out like, "Hey, you should come and talk about your father and sit with these young people and just hear what they have to say. Just hear them out." He said, "I put this panel together. We have over a hundred young boys from different charter schools in New York City, and we're bringing them in one location to talk." So, when I started to hear what they had to say, and they were saying things that I've said before, things that happened with my father's situation or other situations, I'm just looking like, wow! These young people are very edu-cated. So, when I got up to speak, I don't remember exactly what I said. I just spoke from my heart, and it was just like boom, a standing ovation, and then when they came after me they're like, "Your story is so inspiring!" From there, traveling around to different colleges, going to different middle schools. I would say my favorite middle school was Eagle Academy. That was my favorite middle school. We went to go talk to the Phoenix Suns. We've talked to Tina Charles and Swin Cash. I was able to meet all of these people and basically tell them that my voice is of value.

ETAN THOMAS. Hey, listen. You know you got my support, Emerald. Like you said before I think, Angel, you said it, people need to hear from Emerald.

ANGEL MCCOUGHTRY. Yeah!

ETAN THOMAS. You know what I mean. They need to hear everything that she just said. Because that'll put it into a different perspective than for them because they think they understand but they don't really understand. That's why I really applaud all of the work that all of you are doing. I appreciate you all coming on the show.

EMERALD GARNER. Having my daughter and calling my father, "Hey, Dad, can you buy me this?" "Well," he used to say, "you know it's over for you, like you know, I suppose you as a child. Now you have your own child, so tell me what my granddaughter needs." It was like, "Wait hold up, now I really gotta survive." So, it was just like, "Now that's another survival issue, and then I lose my father completely," because although he said, "Oh, I'm only gonna do for Kaylee," I still got what I want anyway. So, it was just like, "OK, now I'm losing my father, so I don't have that trump card in my back pocket like, oh, boom, let me call my dad, oh let me call my dad because I know he's always gonna handle it." So, that now, I had to become a survivor. A survivor on my own because my father was at the top. Building my story around just talking about my father would not work, it would be impossible to get to know me.

I want people to know who I am, my struggles, having to go through my trials and tribulations and still coming out of that as a survivor. Fast forward to losing my sister and taking on her two children. I was already with a six-year-old who was in school out of my face, don't gotta worry about Pampers, and now I have this four-month-old. I'm working full-time. I'm an activist. I'm traveling all over the place. What am I gonna do with this child? I don't even remember how to change Pampers. I had to get accustomed to dealing with that situation. Fast forward to right now. I'm struggling with these children. It's just a lot. I've had to survive so much and I don't want people to think that the worst thing you ever had to deal with in your life is your father getting killed. That's at the top but then I got ten more situations that made me who I am. That molded me into who I am. That taught me how to be who I am.

Like knowing one of my foster parents. I was with her when I was pregnant transitioning into my own apartment. She passed away from COVID. She is one of the people who actually taught me. She's one of the contributors who taught me how to maintain a home, how to maintain it when you get up and go to work every day. No excuses, you got to get it done. If you don't have toilet paper, you can't wipe your butt. You don't get toothpaste, you can't brush your teeth. So, those little gems that were dropped in my life, I want to share them with other people, because I'm not the only person going through it. Like you know George Floyd's daughter is going to grow up. She's going to grow up a lot better, because of the spotlight on her life, she's going to have a better chance of making it out.

ETAN THOMAS. You know, George Floyd really shook up the entire country, and it was interesting because there are a lot of different murders that happened before, but George Floyd had a particular type of effect with America as a whole. Talk about that case in particular and what you thought when you saw everything.

RENEE MONTGOMERY. It was just the way that it happened, you know, and then you hear what the arrest was even for, and it's confusing for that level of aggression, for what he's being arrested for, and so then you just, I've never seen the full clip because I don't want to, but you just see the look on the officer's face, the inhumane look that they have when others are calling out crying out for help and just the way the officers look. Just how the whole thing happened. It just doesn't sit right with you, to watch a man murdered on national television and so, yeah, it was just the circumstances surrounding the case. So, like that many people and then when you find out that those officers had a record and they previously were doing things before. It's just the whole thing as a whole. It just doesn't sit right.

ETAN THOMAS. Thank you, thank you for coming on. This is the type of Martin Luther King Day panel that needs to happen. Have a discussion. Not just, I have a dream. Let's look at it, it was a fantastic speech but let's put it into real terms today and explore how the struggle continues. So, thank you all for what you are doing. Please stay safe. I know y'all are all overseas and everywhere. So, stay safe, and thanks again for coming on *The Rematch*.

◊ ◊ ◊

Being able to share my story and connect with these amazing women was so inspiring for me. They laid their careers on the line to speak out against injustice, and the way they all did it together was something that I really want to do with impacted family members. There really is strength in numbers, and the WNBA shows that time and time again. I love the way they all lift each other up and support each other. People think that different teams have to be at war with each other and genuinely not like each other in order to compete at the highest level against each other. Now, I don't know if all of these women get along or not. I'm sure everyone can't always get along, that's just not how life works. But when it comes time to get things done, they all accord. They all support each other, and that's just absolutely beautiful.

CHAPTER 12

Paying It Forward

It's hard to imagine that I would ever be equipped to help somebody else who has had a loved one taken from them by police, but here I am. The person who couldn't leave my apartment at times, who would wake up screaming like a mad woman from nightmares, who has contemplated suicide, would be counseling other people who are having similar thoughts and struggles. Sometimes, talking with other survivors is just as therapeutic for me as it is for them, but it is something that I have a definite passion to continue doing—it's almost like a calling. This chapter includes interviews I conducted with two different amazingly strong and courageous survivors, Angelique Kearse and Pamela Brooks.

Interview with Angelique Kearse, Widow of Andrew Kearse

We first met at the National Action Network headquarters for the Huddle, and she was brought in by Aries and Ashley Sharpton. I just happened to be at the Huddle that day, and I was sitting in the back just listening. And when I heard her telling her story, it hit me so hard I started getting emotional, and I didn't want to start crying in front of her so I stepped out for a while and tried to collect myself. But everything was so fresh and new for her and it brought back all of the memories for me, so I was really retraumatized. My entire body was literally shaking, even after I stepped out of the space we were in.

But after I collected myself, I was able to go back in and connect with her, and I found out that it was actually her birthday that day, so we talked and went out to eat after the Huddle and just really connected. I had been where she was and I saw myself in her. The whirlwind of emotions, the pain, the anger, the hurt, the sadness, the fear, it was like looking at a younger version of myself. Not younger in age, but younger in going through the process that survivors have to go through. It was at that moment that I knew we were going to join forces in this fight for justice.

I wanted to interview Angelique for this book because I feel that her story is one that not only needs to be told, but the results we were able to achieve by aligning can be modeled by other survivors as there is strength in numbers.

EMERALD GARNER. Hey, Angelique, thank you for being a part of this.

ANGELIQUE KEARSE. You know you don't have to thank me. I told you before, we're in this together.

EMERALD GARNER. Yes we are. So tell everyone how we connected.

ANGELIQUE KEARSE. Well, I knew of you before we met because I knew what happened to your father. So when we actually met, we just connected immediately because what happened to your father happened to my husband. The police took both of them away from us. And another survivor can just relate on a whole different level to another survivor.

EMERALD GARNER. That's definitely true.

ANGELIQUE KEARSE. Sometimes you have family and friends that try to understand, but they can't really understand because it's not their loved one. They may be outraged or angry or upset that it happened, but they can't relate to having nightmares night after night after night, or dreaming that your loved one is alive and you are hugging them or kissing them or they're holding you in their arms only to wake up and realize it was all a dream. They don't know about having the video replay in your dreams like a movie and you wake up drenched in sweat, screaming, crying. They don't know about the depression you feel knowing that you will never see your loved one again while the person who murdered them is just living their best life like nothing happened. They just don't know exactly what that feels like but another survivor does.

EMERALD GARNER. I've had people say to me, "When do you think you will get over it?" or "It's time to move on with your life," and I just want to scream.

ANGELIQUE KEARSE. I have screamed and said a lot of words with the screams when people have said cruel, insensitive mess like that to me. This is an open wound that we can't even imagine ever closing, and only another survivor, at least from my experience, can really understand that.

EMERALD GARNER. I couldn't agree more. And this is from people close to us, we're not even talking about the media.

ANGELIQUE KEARSE. Yeah, the media is a whole other topic, and we know what they are about. But yeah, people close to us like friends, coworkers, family, like people in our circle is what I'm talking about. They can say all the wrong things sometimes but, yeah, that's why we connected immediately.

EMERALD GARNER. Talk about how the media picks and chooses.

ANGELIQUE KEARSE. Yeah, the media just wants to follow headlines and get clicks. They want to go with the hot story. They don't really care about any of us, they just want to exploit our pain for clicks. But what the media also does is ignore what we really want. They wanna ask us if we forgive the cops.

EMERALD GARNER. I hate when they do that. They did that to my mom, and she went off. But that's how she was feeling at that moment, but why would you even ask her that?

ANGELIQUE KEARSE. Because they don't care. They don't express the fact that we all want basically the same things, justice for our loved ones, that they hold all killer cops accountable, and they make the laws so that what happened to our loved one won't happen to anyone else. But they never, or I won't say never, but very rarely tell that story, they don't print that. They wanna ask, do we forgive the cop.

EMERALD GARNER. We also shared about some of the politicians and activists taking advantage of us.

ANGELIQUE KEARSE. Yes, and you kept me so calm on so many occasions because I was actually believing some of them actually cared. They say they're gonna help, and they have the power to help, and it's all talk. Especially the politicians. Now, some do help, but there are a lot that just talk a good game in the public but don't do anything. Same with some of the fake activists. And let me say this, every politician and activist should know the stories within their city. I know you can't know all of the cases all around the country, but you should be able to at least know the stories in your city. Not just the main national headlines like Breonna Taylor or George Floyd or Eric Garner but the ones in your city that have been fighting for years because they all need a voice.

EMERALD GARNER. Because not all of the cases get the same amount of attention.

ANGELIQUE KEARSE. Exactly. That's why I appreciate you sharing your platform with me so many times and helping me get the word out about what happened to my husband because he should still be here with me and his children and they murdered him. [*Starts crying.*] I'm sorry I'mma try not to get emotional and make it through this interview.

EMERALD GARNER. It's OK, you know we can just cry together sometimes because, honestly, that may be what we need to do in that moment.

ANGELIQUE KEARSE. That's what I'm saying, people don't understand that. But yeah, I have heard so many survivors say, "But what about my family?" or "I've been fighting for a decade and haven't gotten one article written on my loved one," or there are some families who don't have a dashcam or a video and no big time attorney picks up their case so they can at least get a settlement. And of course it's not all about the money, but a lot of families have to take up a collection to bury their loved one that the police murdered. While they are dealing with depression, anxiety, mental health issues, and they can't even get help for that either because everything cost money.

EMERALD GARNER. It breaks my heart. OK, tell your story for all of the people who are not familiar with what happened to your husband Andrew.

ANGELIQUE KEARSE. I am the wife of Andrew Kearse. He was thirty-six years old. And on May 11, 2017, he just came home from doing two years and only lasted fifteen days. Andrew pleaded for his life over seventy times in seventeen minutes, stating the same words as Eric Garner and the same words as George Floyd, saying "I can't breathe." And he died one minute before he got to the police station from cardiac arrest. And every moment that Andrew was pleading for his life, he was announcing to the officer every emotion that he was going through and experiencing, and the whole time Officer Mark Weekes is belittling him, mocking him, actually making jokes about him while he is saying that he couldn't breathe—like a serial killer with no empathy. Andrew said, "I feel like throwing up," and Officer Mark Weekes yelled back, "You better not throw up in my car." He's telling him, "I'm getting numb, my chest is hurting," and you can hear this all on the dashcam video. I have had to listen to this too many times that I hear it in my sleep, but Andrew was telling him every symptom he was having of a heart attack, and Officer Mark Weekes took it all as a joke. He drove slow, didn't call for any type of medical assistance, he's making jokes, laughing, mocking him while my husband is literally pleading for his life.

EMERALD GARNER. Just no humanity at all.

ANGELIQUE KEARSE. None, they wouldn't treat an animal that way. If they picked up a dog and was taking the dog to the pound, and the dog started coughing and wheezing, I guarantee you they would've done everything they could to make sure that dog was OK. And I'm not even talking about one of their special police dogs, just a regular stray dog they picked up in the park.

EMERALD GARNER. I've actually seen them treat dogs with so much love and care. And dogs that just attacked someone or bit someone. And they are petting the dog, calming the dog down, they don't even like to tase dogs, I've actually seen them pull out treats to calm a dog down. I'm sorry, I just got triggered, but continue with your story.

ANGELIQUE KEARSE. No that's OK, and I'm right with you on that because they treated my husband a way that they would never treat a dog. They have more value for a dog than they did for Andrew and that hurts me to my soul. And it's not like they don't know what they are supposed to do if someone they apprehended is in distress. Officer

Weeks was trained in the military. He knew what to do, he just chose not to.

EMERALD GARNER. We have such similar stories, it's eerie.

ANGELIQUE KEARSE. I know, so when they got to the station, it took him a while to even get out the car and place him on the concrete. And you see all these officers in Schenectady coming out laughing, joking, drinking coffee while my husband is still not getting any type of medical attention. So finally after a while, a captain went to Mark Weekes and asked him what happened, and he said, "Oh, he was doing that 'I can't breathe' thing all the way here." And the dash cam and everything Andrew went through, I can't get it out my head. I can close my eyes right now and see him crying for his life and hear his voice and see him pleading and them mocking him and treating him with just no human regard. Even talking right now, my hands are shaking, and I am trying not to hyperventilate.

EMERALD GARNER. Oh, well let's take a break because I know how that can be. Let's stop for a moment. [*We take a break.*]

ANGELIQUE KEARSE. OK, I'm sorry, I've been trying to get better at that. I've told the story a few times. I went on *The Breakfast Club*, and talking to reporters, but it never gets easier.

EMERALD GARNER. Girl, you know you don't have to apologize to me. You've seen me break down in the middle of an interview. But it's crazy when the people try to cop an attitude with you because you are getting emotional talking about your husband or your father or loved one who was killed but they're just worried about the story or their precious film rolling or whatever.

ANGELIQUE KEARSE. And what's a horrible reminder is sometimes the media doesn't look at us as humans either, just a topic for their story. But yes, this is why I have been fighting for my husband since he was taken away from me, and I will continue to fight for him. I have to be his voice. He was literally begging for his life. He said, "I beg you please," and he begged for his life over seventy times in seventeen minutes, and he got nothing and nobody should die like that.

EMERALD GARNER. Whew, OK, so let's talk about the Andrew Kearse law and what you were able to accomplish.

ANGELIQUE KEARSE. You mean what *we* were able to accomplish. But yes, in June of last year, we got the Eric Garner law and the Andrew Kearse law passed in New York State that states that if anyone, if any law enforcement officer, doesn't provide medical assistance to people in custody experiencing medical distress, they will be held criminally liable from this day forth. They passed in the Senate the Andrew Kearse Accountability Act. And I have to give a major shout-out to Elizabeth Warren, Ayana Presley, AOC, and there are a couple of other politicians.

EMERALD GARNER. Kirsten Gillibrand and Edward Markey, they were the original cosponsors.

ANGELIQUE KEARSE. Yes, definitely them too, thanks.

And this was on his fourth anniversary, May 11, 2021, and it was reintroduced into the Senate and now we just need it to pass, because it sets a precedent and it will be criminal and civil and they will no longer get away with doing what they did to my Andrew. Also, the United Nations did a report on thirty-seven cases of police brutality in the US, the most horrendous cases, and Andrew was a part of that. He was one of the cases they examined. So this law should've been passed on the federal level, and I don't understand what the hold up is. I am so glad it passed in the State of New York, and that is a big accomplishment for us, because we got the Eric Garner law passed in the State of New York too, but they should both be passed federally so no cop in the country can get away with what they did to my husband and your father.

EMERALD GARNER. I agree 100 percent, but that's why the fight continues and we're not giving up on this. We are going to keep fighting.

ANGELIQUE KEARSE. Yes, and what's crazy is the officer is still on the job. After he murdered Andrew, he took himself off the job, put himself on administrative leave. He then opened a bus company, which was really a slap in my face, he got married, and I was thinking, "Wow, so his wife was walked down the aisle by her father, but my daughters will never be able to be walked down the aisle by their father because you murdered him." Our last daughter was turning two when he was murdered, so she doesn't even get to know her father. Andrew got killed on May 11, and her birthday was May 25. She turned two, so she will barely remember him alive. And he took that away from her, Officer Mark Weekes robbed her of that.

EMERALD GARNER. Talk about the comments made by the chief of police.

ANGELIQUE KEARSE. Oh my God, yes. So last October, the chief of police called me himself after four years of me fighting and grieving and not getting any answers. He tells me that he is publicly announcing that they messed up on Andrew's case, but they were going to keep him on the job. I couldn't believe what I was hearing.

EMERALD GARNER. Talk about the cop's past, because one thing we are seeing in a lot of these cases is that the police officers shouldn't have been police officers in the first place. Either they have a long list of prior complaints of excessive force or violent incidents etc., etc.

ANGELIQUE KEARSE. Yeah, well Weekes definitely shouldn't have been on the job. A few weeks before he murdered Andrew, Weekes was beat up by an MMA fighter. And he was emotionally damaged and stated that he couldn't be around people and was constantly in fear of his life like a paranoia, PTSD type of mental and emotional state. Now, this is all on record. So my question is, why would you have this man carrying a gun and a badge and having the authority and the power that comes along with that police uniform? You can't just give anyone power like that, because the wrong people, it could be really dangerous for them to have that type of power.

EMERALD GARNER. Ridiculous. Now during this process, you actually wrote Weekes on social media, and he wrote you back. Tell me that story.

ANGELIQUE KEARSE. So, I messaged him on Facebook, and his reply was that, he said that after the attorney general finished their report, that he will speak to me and answer all of my questions. When the attorney general and the grand jury failed to indict him, he blocked me without saying a word to me. So he robbed me of the opportunity to confront him, and I needed that. I feel that every survivor should sit down with their killer cop just like when they have the victim's statements. I want to sit down with him, have him explain to me his side, what happened, what he was thinking, why he chose, I want to hear him say it directly to me, and I think he owes me that explanation. My children will probably need that for themselves as well. Me and Andrew have four children together, and none of them know anything but what they read as far as articles and the dashcam, which just shows the actual murder. And this man just gets to go about his life like nothing happened? Like he didn't take my Andrew's life? That's not fair, and I don't see how he can live with himself with that. OK, I'm getting emotional again, I may need to take another break.

EMERALD GARNER. It's OK, it's OK. Let's just stop for now, and let me give you a hug and I just want to let you know that your strength and your courage is amazing. And we are going to be in this fight together, you hear me? I have your back. And if you need to cry or vent or need a rider to go march with you or we need to get back on a big Zoom call with all the politicians to push for these bills and new bills to be passed, I'm here for you. We have to stick together and continue this fight because what these cops are doing, they are ruining lives. They are traumatizing lives. They are breaking down family units and structures. My dad was the patriarchal head of our family. I know a lot of people use that word *patriarchy* like it's a bad thing, but he was the head, and after he was removed we all started to crumble. The whole family. He was the glue that kept us all together. So I am in this fight with you. I mean that. You started the Andrew Kearse Foundation, and I am so excited to see all you're going to do with that, so just know you have a sister for life.

ANGELIQUE KEARSE. You don't know how much that means to me. Thank you.

Interview with Pamela Brooks, Mother of Amir Brooks

As soon as I read about Amir Brooks's case, my heart grew heavy. I actually started hyperventilating. He was only seventeen years old. You haven't lived any type of life yet at just seventeen. It was a case of mistaken identity, where the cop thought he was involved in a series of robberies, so they chased him on his dirt bike. He lost control of his bike and crashed into a tree.

This happened in DC. I was introduced to Amir's mother by Etan who connected with Ms. Brooks through an activist by the name of Jamilia Land. I didn't know how this conversation would go, since I had never actually met Ms. Brooks before. What was I going to say to her? What if she was angry and took it out on me? What if I asked a question the wrong way and accidentally traumatized her or triggered her the way I have been traumatized and triggered by reporters so often? I had so many fears going into this interview, and I actually tried to get Etan to do the interview with me, but he said, "No, you're ready to do this by yourself. You don't need me." We had done so many events together, I may have been using him as a crutch, or maybe more of a safety net because I knew that if I did ever feel as though I needed to pause or compose myself, or take a step back, he could start talking until I gathered my composure, but I was glad he pushed me to do this interview solo. And I was amazed to hear Ms. Brooks's story and again connect with another survivor in this struggle.

EMERALD GARNER. Thank you for joining another episode of *Justice Pursuit with Emerald Garner*. I have the wonderful Ms. Pamela Brooks here. She is the mother of Amir Brooks. I would like for her to introduce herself and tell us a little bit about her story. I'm so glad that you could be with us. Good morning, welcome, sending love and light from me to you. Good morning.

PAMELA BROOKS. Good morning. Thank you so much for having me, and it's a pleasure meeting you. My name is Pamela Brooks. My son's name is Amir Brooks. On August 4, 2014, Amir and his cousin were riding a dirt bike. And this police officer thought they were someone else. And they chased my son, he chased my son on a dirt bike on the wrong side of the street into incoming traffic on the highway. This police officer was off duty. He chased my son from out of Maryland into Washington, DC. And my son's cousin, who was also on the bike, told me that the police was bumping the bike. And to make a long story short, my son lost control and hit a tree, and he crashed.

And this police officer left my son on the street like an animal. Didn't help him. After my son crashed, it shows on tape this police officer getting out of his car, seeing my son and his cousin on the street, he got back in the car and pulled off. He didn't help them. He went back. . . Let me go back a little bit. At the time, this police officer was working in my apartment complex where I was living previously. He was doing the part-time thing, doing security. So your business is to stay on the complex and handle what's going on around here. You're not on "police duty," right. After he left my son, he went back to the apartment complex and did his little log. This was about time for him to get off work. He wrote on the log that he chased a bike, but the bike fled into DC. And that was it, period. Nothing else.

EMERALD GARNER. Never mentioned the accident, never mentioned that he was hurt. And that's horrible. I just have to say, I know you're tired of hearing it because I'm tired of hearing it. But I have to give you my condolences, because I have a daughter, and I could only imagine getting a phone call saying she's out riding her bike and then she never comes back. So I definitely understand. And we go through these things where we're not seen of value, or as person, or as valuable. But Amir was valuable, and he was a human being, and he deserved the right to be treated as a human being. He was your heart, he was a lot of people's hearts. So the fact that he was taken away from us, and my father and my sister were taken away from us, as a direct result of police brutality. Everybody hears the headlines, everybody hears what's going on, they read the stories, but they never understand what we go through in the background. And a part of this platform is letting people know that we have feelings too. So please just tell us a little bit about how your life dynamic has changed and also if Amir has any siblings.

PAMELA BROOKS. Yes, it changed my life drastically, because, I'm not sure if you knew this, my son died three weeks after your dad.

EMERALD GARNER. Oh wow, I didn't know that.

PAMELA BROOKS. Yeah, and three days before Michael Brown.

EMERALD GARNER. Wow.

PAMELA BROOKS. It was back-to-back. We had seen and discussed everything we saw on the news about your dad. We had a full family discussion. We were all devastated for you. We were outraged for you. We cried for you. And while we were making the arrangements for my son's funeral, I see on the news about Michael Brown being killed. So it was back-to-back.

But it has changed my entire life drastically and the life of my family forever. The first year, I was a mess. The first couple years, it was absolutely horrible. I couldn't even get out of my house to speak, I definitely couldn't talk about it like this. Right now, I'm doing so much better. You just never know what hand you're going to be dealt. You think you have this life that you're going to see your kids grow old, have grandchildren, and then in the blink of an eye, they're taken away from you.

We're not supposed to bury our children. That's just not the way God intended it to be. And from that day, after losing my son, I started having so many health issues going on. I gained eighty pounds after my son died. Thank God I lost seventy-five of it, but COVID gave me a little bit back. But

I mean, my life completely changed behind this. And Amir was my youngest child, he was the baby, and they took him from me. [*Breaks down crying.*]

EMERALD GARNER. It's OK, take your time, let it out. They say crying is good for the soul, so don't be afraid to let it out.

PAMELA BROOKS. Thank you for saying that. It's just tough sometimes. But, I have two older children, my son, he was seventeen at the time. So like I said, this is six years ago, he would have been twenty-four. He would have turned twenty-four in January, this past January 15. Same birthday as Dr. Martin Luther King Jr.

EMERALD GARNER. Wow, but it's great that you are now able to talk about it. It's not good to keep it all bottled up inside, and I am speaking from experience. I was thrust into it. And because it was so mainstream, I just felt like I had to get the story out. So I didn't worry about my mental health or the time I actually needed to process. So I would be in the bed for days at a time, and at the time that my father passed away, I was a manager at Payless. So I was calling out, and you're the manager, you cannot call out. You need to be there. You are the leader of this team. You are keeping this ship. . . You're keeping the store open. So you're coming to work. And it was just like, I would be at work, and people are talking about it like, "Oh, did you hear about this? Did you hear about that?" And I can't tell the customers not to talk about it, because I don't even want them to know who I am. And if I tell them, "That's my father you're talking about," they're going to ask me questions. So I know exactly how you feel. It's pressure. And then when everything happened with my sister, she was so distraught, she wasn't taking care of her health. And then she also died, she had a massive heart attack at twenty-seven. So we deal with a lot, and then nobody understands that this is literally every day for us. But I want you and all of the other survivors to know and understand that it does get better. It's a process, but it gets better.

PAMELA BROOKS. Yeah, it's definitely a process and it takes time. I thank God I didn't completely lose my mind to be honest, because that could have easily happened. But I will say that everyone grieves differently and people have to take their time and grieve in whatever way they need to, of course as long as you're not hurting yourself or being destructive, which can very easily happen. But whatever time you need, then that's the time you need. People act like there is a time limit to grief, and that's just not true. I am sure I'm going to have triggers for the rest of my life. Every time I see a motorcycle, I see my son and how he used to smile and love riding his motorcycle. I literally see him on the motorcycle when I pass someone today. So yes, I am doing better in my grieving process, but I am definitely still grieving.

EMERALD GARNER. And you have every right to grieve however you need to grieve. I think that's so important. Some people make you feel guilty for grieving. In some cases they don't mean to, but that's still what they do.

PAMELA BROOKS. Oh, I have definitely experienced that. I have had to end some relationships because of that. Also, have had to put some relationships on pause which is what I needed to do for my well being.

EMERALD GARNER. I definitely understand that. There's another thing that I wanted to talk to you about was, when we had our conversation, you mentioned confronting the officer. And I just want to say that is amazing. Because I sat in the courtroom for about two weeks with the officer who killed my father, Pantaleo, and I felt that if I confronted him, I would go to jail, because I want to yell, I want to scream, I want to tell him a lot and I didn't get my chance. So I'm living vicariously through you. Can you walk me through how you confronted the officer?

PAMELA BROOKS. It was just crazy because actually while all this stuff was going on with the court and everything, I never wanted to see this man. Because I know how I was probably going to snap. All my emotions were going to come out.

EMERALD GARNER. And you are entitled to have your feelings without people judging you. No judgment.

PAMELA BROOKS. Yeah, but I knew I wouldn't be able to control it. I know myself. So a lot of times, when I was due to be in court, my sister would go in my place, because I can talk about my son all day long, but when it comes to that court part, it breaks me down. I just can't do it. I just can't. So it was maybe, I think it was three years ago, it was closer to my son's heavenly anniversary. So a friend of mine said, "Come on, let's go out." We went to see Jill Scott at the MGM at the National Harbor. So I was like, "I needed this, I needed to get out." Because around that time, somebody always was like, "Let's go do something." Right. So we're leaving out of the concert hall, and walking into the casino, because I had to get through the casino to get back to my car.

So MGM, they have their security, then they have regular police officers at the door checking IDs. So I just happen to walk by and I said. . . You know how you think you see somebody but you don't see them. So I backed up, I said, "I know this ain't this so-and-so right here." I looked at my phone, because I've got a picture on my phone of him, I keep it. And he was a Black police officer, that's why it hurt me the most. He was Black. I'm like, "We are seeing all of this happen with white cops but this Black so-and-so murdered my son in cold blood and treated him like he wasn't even a human being. Someone who could've looked like his son."

EMERALD GARNER. Wow, yeah, that's a really different dynamic.

PAMELA BROOKS. Yeah, and so I had my phone. So I flipped it up, I told my friend, I just said, "Look at this phone and tell me if you see this person standing over there." And she said, "Yeah, he's right there." Then she said, "Oh my God." She instantly knew who it was. So I said, "This bastard!" He was just out there walking around, laughing, working, looking at women as they passed by and acting like ain't nothing happening, like he didn't murder my son. And this was the first time I ever actually saw him since my son passed. So I had all of this emotion building up inside of me. It was like rumbling like a volcano. I was ready to completely explode.

EMERALD GARNER. Wow, I can't imagine. So then what happened?

PAMELA BROOKS. So, he locked eyes on me, and he immediately put his head down. Like he was in shame. He knew exactly who I was. I could tell how he looked at me. You've heard the expression that someone had a look on their face like they had seen a ghost? Well that's the look he had on his face.

EMERALD GARNER. Wow, this is so intense. I have had so many dreams about meeting Pantaleo face-to-face. I'm sure he has visited your page on social media. I'm sure he knows exactly who you are.

PAMELA BROOKS. That's why I keep my page public on all social media, because I want him to see what he took away from me. And my Amir was a sweet boy, he wasn't no thug in the street. So I walked up to him, and I looked him in his eyes and I said, "Wow, I didn't know MGM had child murderers working here." So my friend was like, "Pam, stop." And I turned to her and said, "You need to leave me alone right now, because if this was your son who was killed, and you saw his killer, you don't know how you would act." And she stepped back.

So he looked at me, and there were three other regular police there. It was him and two other guys. So I looked at him dead in his face and said, "How could you live with yourself? You left a child on the damn street like an animal." I said, "You left my son on the street like an animal. How do you live with yourself?" And the entire time, he was looking down at the ground.

EMERALD GARNER. He couldn't bring himself to look at you, huh?

PAMELA BROOKS. No he couldn't. Had shame all over his face. So I said, "You killed my son." I said, "How do you think I'm feeling?" I said, "Do you understand what you did to my family? The pain and heartache you caused?" So then another friend of mine walked up to me, put her hand on my shoulder. She was like, "Pam, calm down, calm down," but I wasn't trying to hear any of them. This was the moment I had been dreaming of. Seeing my son's killer face-to-face.

EMERALD GARNER. So all this time, he doesn't say a word or look at you?

PAMELA BROOKS. No, eyes stuck to the floor, almost like he was frozen and couldn't move. Then two other officers started walking toward me, and they had their hands on their side, next to their guns. So not on their guns, but right next to it. So I backed away and called my son's friends, and I'm like, "Get to the MGM." But it was by the grace of God nobody replied back.

EMERALD GARNER. They knew that you were just feeling out of emotion, but you were calling them like, "Listen, something needs to happen right now."

PAMELA BROOKS. No, no, the MGM service is bad and it didn't go through until I got out.

EMERALD GARNER. Oh, OK. So God was like, "No, not today." I think he touched your phone service and was like, "You ain't getting nothing today."

PAMELA BROOKS. Because as soon as I left the MGM my son called and was like, "Mom, where you at? Where you at?" I said, "I'm gone now." Because then it's too late. But I told him that after I said what I said to him, the other police officers started walking toward me. And then I looked at Brandon Peters, that's the cop's name, Brandon Peters.

EMERALD GARNER. Brandon Peters. Yes, Brandon Peters the murderer.

PAMELA BROOKS. Yes. So he told the other cops, "Leave her alone." He stopped them. Why did you stop them? Because you knew you were wrong. And from that day forward, and I must say, I got a little bit of peace. Because it got off my heart, and I wanted that man to know how I felt. And after seeing him, I know that he's not sleeping good at night. I know it's weighing on him and haunting him. I can tell, I mean, he couldn't even look at me. Like I said there was nothing but shame all over his expression.

EMERALD GARNER. Wow, I just wanna say how much I admire you. Do you understand how much strength that took to do that? I just think it's so courageous of you to confront the murderer of your son. And going forward, that's what I want to do with this platform is basically tell the stories of the survivors through our eyes. Because they only see what goes on in the media, and that's not everything. They read an article or two and think that they know us. And a lot of the times, we get left behind where it's like, you hear all these people talking about your loved one, but you're still sitting at home in your feelings, in your thoughts, in your emotions. So please just let us know some of the things that you are working on, some of the initiatives that you want to bring to the social justice movement, how we can support you.

PAMELA BROOKS. Well, I've been sitting on a lot of different things. I want to eventually start my son's foundation, the Amir Brooks Foundation. But right now, I just started the No Change Movement. I got that in my LLC. And what I want to do with the No Change Movement, in May of 2019, I became a certified grief coach.

EMERALD GARNER. Wow, congratulations.

PAMELA BROOKS. Thank you. And because there was just so many mothers reaching out to me who had lost children. I was like, "Hmm, I can try to talk to them, but am I saying the right things? Even though I'm grieving myself, am I saying the right thing to them?" So I took this course, and I got my certification. So that's what I want the No Change Movement business part to be about, going out, helping people get through grief. Because this is a tough thing, and the truth is, you can go through these courses all day long with people that are paid to do that. But they don't really understand unless they've gone through it themselves.

EMERALD GARNER. They don't know, and they have no idea.

PAMELA BROOKS. Right, they don't understand. But I don't fault them, they can't understand. So what I wanted to do is bring awareness to these police officers like, this chasing thing, in Maryland, in DC. DC has a strict no-chase policy. But see, in my son's case, this police officer was an off-duty

Maryland cop that chased him, and this happened in DC. So DC didn't even touch it.

EMERALD GARNER. Right, and it's just unfortunate that you have elected officials. You have people who want to say they're there for the people. But then as soon as we bring you a situation where a mother has lost her son at the hands of a cop, you say that you can't touch it. And that's the problem with a lot of these elected officials, they campaign to say that they're with us. But when they get in the office, they turn their backs on us.

PAMELA BROOKS. Exactly.

EMERALD GARNER. So that's another issue. And I definitely want to support you in the grief counseling. I just put out a public post on social media basically telling people that if they have been victims of police brutality, or they're feeling hurt by police brutality to give me a call. I've gotten maybe one or two calls. But I'm definitely going to take the grief counseling certification so that way I know exactly how to handle these calls.

PAMELA BROOKS. The course I took, it's crazy, I Googled it, I was like, "Who do I go to?" And it's crazy that the lady in the course I took, she's right here in DC. But she does it virtual. So people were on there from California. She doesn't have a big group, it's maybe six or seven of us, but it's a lot for me to start. And she was absolutely excellent.

EMERALD GARNER. Yes, and I think that a part of our healing would be telling our story and paying it forward to another person. Because unfortunately, we're still going to have police brutality until we change the laws, we change our police training, we change the dynamic of African American communities and policing. So until we start to change that, I think that a good start is offering grief counseling, because my brother, he never took grief counseling, he didn't talk to anybody, and he's backed up. Not mentally backed up, but as far as his emotions, he caught in this whirlwind of feelings. He's angry, sad, hurt, pissed, but he's a man, and he doesn't know how to express his anger and be respected for his anger. And it's different for men. It's different for us too don't get me wrong. The "angry Black woman" stigma is definitely a thing, but Black men are just so much more threatening even when they are calm. That's just reality. So my brother, he has all these emotions but he has to be so careful with his presentation and no that's not fair but it's reality. But people unfortunately have to be taught how to navigate that reality.

PAMELA BROOKS. Yeah.

EMERALD GARNER. Survivors have to be taught that you are going to get asked the question if you hate all cops over and over again. Now, yes we all have the right to feel how we want to feel. I never said I hate all police and never will. But that one person Daniel Pantaleo, who caused so much trauma and pain in my life, I lost my father, then I lost my sister. So yes, I hate this guy. But you should respect how I feel. No, I don't want to hate him and kill him, because that's the worst thing that you can do. But I just want to hate him and let people know that this person is a murderer. Your family, your kids, he had a baby, you will know that your father is a murderer. That officer out there, that Black officer, who took your baby from you, his kids, his wife, everybody needs to know that he's a murderer.

PAMELA BROOKS. That's for sure. And that's my thing, my son, my oldest son, he's the same way. He's just mad. My daughter, she's twenty-six, she really doesn't talk. She just can't, because they were so close. I can't get her to come to events, it's too painful. She said, "I'll get there one day, but I just can't do it because I don't want to be around all that crying."

EMERALD GARNER. Right. Well, I'm offering an olive branch if she would like to talk. And if I can support her, it doesn't have to be on the platform, it doesn't have to be anywhere. She can call my phone, I will call her. I will be on her like, "Hello, you up? You can call me." Because that's what people did for me. If I'm calling two or three in the morning crying, they know that it's either my father or my sister. It's not I'm calling you three in the morning to chitchat. No, because I know you sleep. So I'm calling you to wake you up because I'm feeling a certain way, and you offered that to me. And my friends have always come through for me. So I'm offering that olive branch to your daughter and your son, and even to you in regard to your process if you ever want to talk, have a conversation, yell, scream. I wanted to create this thing called the destruction room where you just go and break stuff, because I found that to be very therapeutic. So I'm really trying to form a group of us so we can have our peace of mind, we can also live comfortably, because I'm sure going to work is hard, having to look for a job and hear people talk about your son, that is hard, that is very hard. And a lot of people get a lot of funding for their organizations. And then people like us who have been through it, we don't get the type of support for our organizations.

So I'm breaking barriers with this, and somebody is going to find your program, somebody is going to fund your grief counseling, and I'm putting it out into the atmosphere, and I'm manifesting that all of our nonprofits will take off just as much as the major organizations who do it because they just want to support the family. We're doing it because we are the family. And we have a story, and we all have a story. So let's be the voice for our loved ones. I definitely want to continue this conversation moving forward. Maybe we could start grief counseling together, virtual grief counseling, whatever it is, to help another mother, sister, brother, cousin, friend. Because not only the siblings are affected, his friends are affected too. What about them? His teammates. Everybody. Even your daughter, her friends. I'm sure they knew him, they see their friend breaking down, it affects them as well. So it's a bunch of people that we need to be concerned about even beyond the immediate family.

PAMELA BROOKS. So, my mom has since passed away, and I know my mother died of grief because of the grief. Her pastor came to us and told us, he said, "You know your mom grieved your son's death to her death. And it killed her to see her grandchild like that, it's killing her to see you like that and she couldn't do nothing to take that pain away from you." And it just broke my heart. And I know you experienced the same thing with your sister.

EMERALD GARNER. Oh my God, I'm trying so hard to not completely break down right now after hearing you say that.

PAMELA BROOKS. Well like you said, we can break down together and lift each other up together, because I'm sure we both have moments of breaking down and needing someone's help.

EMERALD GARNER. You have no idea. I'm so tired of losing loved ones because of this situation. And a lot of people contemplate suicide. I have, myself.

PAMELA BROOKS. I have too.

EMERALD GARNER. I'm sure we all have at one point or another after our family was killed. People really have no idea. But yes, we all need to support each other. And I think that we could do a better job at supporting each other. We have to build our safety net, because everybody else has a safety net and we need to build ours, we need to structure our story, our narrative, and our legacy. Because after everything is said and done, only you know Amir's story, only I know my father's story, only I know Erica's story, because we are them and they are us. So we just have to continue with the togetherness.

PAMELA BROOKS. Definitely, but what I want to also say before I leave is, I want people to get involved before it hits home, I want people to get involved before it's a high-profile case, because there are a lot more cases that consistently happen that you never hear about. People just hear the high-profile cases. So don't wait for it to happen to you to get involved. If you see someone going through something that they may need your support in a march, go support them. Don't just support the high-profile cases that are all over the news and are being covered and trending and the hot item everyone is paying attention to. If it's a local person, support that family, because they definitely need you, because these police are out of control. And it's going to continue to happen, unfortunately.

EMERALD GARNER. Right. And we have to start building those bridges to change it. Also, and I really want to keep reiterating this point, we have to support each other. If we know somebody who's affected by police brutality in our neighborhood, we should definitely check in on them, we should not isolate them. We should not throw them to the wolves. We should just bring them in and support them, because unfortunately, a lot of times, people get involved for the wrong reasons.

PAMELA BROOKS. Amen. I have experienced and heard so many horror stories

EMERALD GARNER. Exactly, we all have. So we want to make sure that we let everybody know that support us. And I say us because I'm a part of that community. And I need support, Ms. Pam needs support. Everybody needs support. So differences aside, because we see all the organizations, the activist communities, a lot of them don't work together.

PAMELA BROOKS. I've noticed that too.

EMERALD GARNER. It's not about ego or anything else. We need change. And we need people fighting for that change. We don't have anything to do with the beef that they have. I don't have anything to do with anything that they dealt with in the past, I am a person looking for help and looking for assistance. So that's how I want to go forward with it. I don't be in the middle of rivalry organizations, because I think everybody is working toward the same goal, so we all should be working together. But that's just not the case. So we have to start building our bridges. And we need to connect on ourself, and build a platform for ourself. So when it's time to talk about Amir, they call you. When it's time to talk about Eric Garner, they call me, and they don't call the activist or organization who doesn't even know me from a can of paint. And then they're talking about my situation like they actually know me. So that pattern has to stop.

PAMELA BROOKS. I just think you are so amazing, and I am so glad we connected and I can't wait until my daughter gets to a place where she can start speaking like you. But she'll get there.

EMERALD GARNER. Hey, it was a process for me. I wasn't always this way at all. So tell your daughter, we will figure it out. I've been through a tremendous journey. So many struggles. And so many people have helped me and so many people have tried to take advantage of me. I've lost friends and family members, and I'm not talking about them no longer being on this earth anymore, we have just splintered apart. There are so many cautionary tales I want to tell new survivors about because I've been through it all. How the settlement splinters the family. People say funerals bring out the worst of people, you can't imagine what settlement money does. But yes, now it is time for me to continue the fight for justice by paying it forward, and that's exactly what I am going to do.

CHAPTER 13

We Can't Breathe

We Can't Breathe (www.wecantbreathe.net) is an organization I created in remembrance of my father and my sister. As I have said, and as I'll always repeat, during this journey after my father was taken away from me, mental health was not provided us, and it should have been. The protocol with murders by the police is always: the person is killed, everyone is up in arms initially, their name is a trending hashtag, people march and protest, the family does media, the cops usually get off or are not even charged, and then everyone moves on to the next case. So I wanted to break the cycle of coming into a family's life for a moment, and then going away.

I hired an amazing woman by the name of JoHanna "J" Thompson who has really been a godsend. I have expressed some of the issues with people taking advantage of impacted family members and being in this for the wrong reasons, so when I connected with J and saw her passion, selflessness, and ingenuity mixed with intelligence, brilliance, and Black excellence, I saw that she was the ideal director of development and fundraising for We Can't Breathe.

We got a grant from the Melinda French Gates Foundation called Pivotal Ventures, another grant from CJI (Circle for Justice Innovations), and a fiscal sponsorship from the Global Fund for Women. We now had the infrastructure set for my foundation. So when we revamped our organization, we decided to lead with the mission that We Can't Breathe Inc.'s mission is to eliminate all forms of police violence and heal traumatic adverse experiences through local and global education, community dialogue, and policy advocacy. We demand this stops today to advocate for not one more person lost to police violence and the punitive carceral systems established across the globe. We believe police violence is not a white vs. Black vs. "blue" argument—it is everyone standing against institutional racism collectively.

We are the children of the movement, a youth-led and centered justice project building an intergenerational and intersectional movement. We hold the institutions, created to provide safety and enforce the law, accountable to the people as we disrupt the reckless reign of terror in all communities—without recourse—and the overcriminalization of marginalized communities. We believe that #BlackMindsMatter and we focus on mental health rooted in restorative healing while advocating for policies "with teeth" to meet the needs of every person to live free from fear.

So we came up with what we're calling the Justice Project, which focuses on mental health, job security, and civil rights education. Specifically concerning mental health, we are doing the Hearts of Justice program which offers counseling for youth after 5:00 p.m. as well as a twenty-four hour rotating schedule of wraparound services.

I started off with two youths to pilot the program, and we have grown significantly since then. I want to eventually be able to serve hundreds and hundreds of youth, but of course that takes even more funding and resources. So the way the program is set up, when the youth enter, they receive four weeks of mental health support. We set them up with a clinician, whether it's a therapist or substance abuse counselor, but somebody who is certified to be on call for them. So, they would enter the program, they would sign up for the therapy sessions, and by week four, the therapist, job coach, and myself would determine what the specific needs are for this specific youth. One of the problems is that people often use a cookie cutter or a standard protocol that they have learned should be used across the board. But everyone is different, and the therapy has to be tailor-made to them in particular, and you have to learn them before you can prescribe what would be best for them.

So back to our pilot with our two students. We began to meet with them weekly, we have people like myself who made themselves available around the clock twenty-four hours to them, and one of the students was not doing well emotionally, spiritually, physically. I had her meet with my senior adviser and a mentorship coordinator at ACS, who I wanted to bring in for counselor support as she already had the certifications, and we met with both of them for four weeks.

I took the two students to the Huddle under the leadership of Ashley Sharpton, and I always refer back to the Huddle because I benefited so much from going there, and I still go there on Monday nights as often as I can. And I can bring my youth with me there as well. Group therapy is so beneficial. You can go and speak if you want to, and if you choose to sit in silence and just listen to everyone else, you can do that as well. You don't feel as though you are alone in whatever you are dealing with. You also hear testimonies from people who may have been doing worse off than you are, and you get to hear how they made it through and how they were able to overcome their obstacles. Being able to see that there is a possibility of a light at the end of the tunnel is crucial, because it gives you hope.

You also have the ability to connect with other people who are struggling or dealing or going through their healing process. Again, that's how I connected with Angelique Kearse, and we became not only friends who leaned on each other, but we started working together on projects to help other people, which served as part of our healing process. I can't say enough how beneficial group therapy is.

So I took the students there to the Huddle after doing the mental health and the basic needs assessment. We identified that one of them was in dire need of extensive mental health therapy, and just simply getting her a job was not going to fulfill her needs. She needed to focus on mental health before she did anything else. The other was able to secure weekly therapy, and she was able to secure finances for her basic needs. We connected her with an organization called Queen's Defenders to provide those basic needs like food, phone bill, and part-time job, while we continued to figure out what direction she wants to go in her life. We were able to discover that she wanted to go back to school for nursing to become a birth doula. So with those two pilot cases, we developed an entire program that focuses on mental health, we figure out the basic needs, which serves as a transition period before we get them completely on their feet and set up with an actual job. In the meantime, we are working with their healing process and getting them the help they need mentally, emotionally, and spiritually so they can get back on their feet and into society and lead a productive and healthy life.

I am providing what I wish my family and I would've had. This is what I needed and what every member of my family needed. All of us. I know what it feels like to not be heard, for nobody to understand where I am coming from or what I am really feeling. Or having people express that they wanted to help and that they felt bad for me, but what I really needed was something they couldn't help me with. And I didn't know how to express to them what I really needed. So now I am in a position to pay it forward and give these youths the help that I wish I would've had.

Another aspect that is of the utmost importance is to be consistent. So when I took my youths to the Huddle, the first thing they asked was, "Will this be available every week?" A lot of times with therapy, help, and programs, the consistency is missing and everything that you gained has the potential to completely fall apart because the consistency wasn't there. In most traditional therapy setups, you can only speak to your therapist on the specific days you are scheduled. So at We Can't Breathe, we focus on twenty-four hour wraparound services, meaning you can call your person any hour of the day if need be and they will be available to you. We won't tell you to make an appointment during business hours, we will be available when you need us. If a youth is in crisis, it's an all-hands-on-deck situation because that's what's needed.

Let me explain what it means when a person is in crisis. A lot of people don't fully understand the severity of a youth being in crisis, but I do because I have experienced it. This is why the best person to have as a sponsor if you are addicted to alcohol is typically someone who is a recovering alcoholic. The best person to have for someone who is addicted to drugs is someone who is a recovering drug addict. I am someone who had consistent moments of crisis in the middle of the night, whether it was having nightmares, replaying seeing my father being killed, closing my eyes and seeing Daniel Pantaleo smiling and walking around enjoying his life, police laughing at me and taunting me, being afraid, having dreams of myself being choked to death the way my father was, waking up in cold sweats, being unable to control my breathing, being so upset I wanted to punch a hole in the wall, I could go on and on. And a lot of times, these thoughts and feelings come in the middle of the night when your mind is most vulnerable, when you have nothing else to escape your thoughts. During the day you can sometimes busy yourself with things of the day, whether it's people, TV, work, kids, etc., but at night, when you're asleep, there is nowhere to hide your thoughts, nothing to protect you from your nightmares, no barrier to hide you from your triggers that haunt you while you are sleeping like Freddy Krueger or something. I know this because for so many years this was my reality almost every night, and I would wake up in crisis.

But it's important to understand that crisis looks different with different people. And some people can experience something that would be a crisis for one person but for another person it's not a big deal and they can recover from it, and this is another problem because a lot of people discount what someone's crisis is because they can't wrap their minds around it being a big deal. For some people, having a bad dream wouldn't be a crisis. They would wake up, realize they were dreaming, get a drink of water, and go back to sleep. For others, they would be awake but still living in the dream in real time, like an army veteran who is awakened by a nightmare that they are at war and they wake up and swing on their spouse or choke them. It's because they are still in their dream and can't separate dream from reality.

Let me give you some examples, there are youths who will be in complete crisis if they experience a break up from their boyfriend after they have emotionally attached to this person and suppressed a trauma they experienced earlier in their lives and found their peace with their boyfriend. So a breakup may not be a big deal to some people, but for this person it's devastating.

Or if a youth learns of a technique to soothe her that she uses on her phone, they have all kinds of soothing apps they recommend nowadays that kids use, and they wake up to use the app and their Internet isn't working for some reason, they might go into panic mode. They may run into the street frantically trying to connect to the Internet because they have developed this system that has now been interrupted or prohibited. Now for most people, waking up and the Internet not working wouldn't be a big deal, but for this person it would send them into a crisis.

There are kids in foster care, like I was for a while growing up. And they're in a home where they get into an argument with their foster parents, and the agency won't come to remove that child or send people in to do conflict resolution but they are in a crisis. And sometimes, not all the time but sometimes, foster children are in a home where they were ripped away from their parents, sometimes split up from their siblings, and you are told that this is the best "environment" for you, and you get there and you're ignored. They don't buy food, they don't treat you like you're a part of the family. You're just there to occupy space and get them a check. And in the middle of the night, when you're supposed to be sleeping before you have to get up and go to school, anger is boiling over at your situation. You're thinking, "My real mother may have been doing X, Y, Z, but I would rather be there than where I am now with people I don't know," and you have no support system and you're lying there with your eyes open and you have bad thoughts, you're in a crisis, and you need to talk to someone right then no matter if it's 3:00 a.m. or not.

Or if a youth wakes up in the middle of the night and hears a noise. If you're in the city, you hear noises all night. Car horns, sirens, people yelling, music, all kinds of stuff. Well, for a person who experienced their father being killed by the police, and they're in a peaceful sleep, what do you think happens to them if they are awakened to the sound of police sirens?

I could go on and on with examples, but I think you get the point. A crisis is a situation where you need to immediately talk to somebody and be taken out of the environment that you're in, whether it's physically, mentally, emotionally, or spiritually. So while crises can present themselves in many different ways, having someone to talk to when your mind is spiraling, when your emotions are completely out of control, when you're having bad thoughts, you need someone to talk to right then and there. It's crucial.

Let me paint a clear picture of what a crisis looks like and how it can manifest, and again, I know about all of this firsthand, I am speaking from experience, not as something I just learned in a textbook, although I have studied this extensively in preparation for the work I am currently doing, but I went through all of this after my father was killed.

Right now, the numbers for teenage bodily harm are through the roof. According to the Mayo Clinic:

Nonsuicidal self-injury, often simply called self-injury, is the act of deliberately harming your own body, such as cutting or burning yourself. It's typically not meant as a suicide attempt. Rather, this type of self-injury is a harmful way to cope with emotional pain, intense anger, and frustration.

While self-injury may bring a momentary sense of calm and a release of tension, it's usually followed by guilt and shame and the return of painful emotions. Although life-threatening injuries are usually not intended, with self-injury comes the possibility of more-serious and even fatal self-aggressive actions.

. . .

The mix of emotions that triggers self-injury is complex. For instance, there may be feelings of worthlessness, loneliness, panic, anger, guilt, rejection, self-hatred or confused sexuality.

. . .

Self-injury can cause a variety of complications, including:
- Worsening feelings of shame, guilt and low self-esteem
- Infection, either from wounds or from sharing tools
- Permanent scars or disfigurement
- Severe, possibly fatal injury
- Worsening of underlying issues and disorders, if not adequately treated.[6]

I have had youth who hurt themselves because they don't feel anything. Nobody is making them feel anything whatsoever. Usually when you grow up in a home, you grow up with love. You are secure in the knowledge that you can always go back home and get support from your mother or father, but for somebody like some of my youths who don't have their parents or age out of foster care, they don't have that. They don't get to go back home and get the support of their father, which for girls is of the utmost importance (speaking from experience), so when that is taken away, you're scrambling to find something or someone to make you feel that comfort. To soothe yourself. Calm yourself. And people turn to all types of vices to do that whether it's drinking, smoking weed, having sex with a lot of people, getting in toxic relationships that they have absolutely no business in, these are all self-comforting techniques because you are grasping at straws to find anything that works. Even if it's actually harming you.

So what we do is we provide a network of support for youth so that they have someone to lean on so that they don't resort to these tactics.

According to the Mayo Clinic, "although self-injury is not usually a suicide attempt, it can increase the risk of suicide because of the emotional problems that trigger self-injury. And the pattern of damaging the body in times of distress can make suicide more likely."

I have had so many youths who have suicidal thoughts. There are certain trigger words or phrases that you hear such as: "I don't know if I can do this," "I can't get out of my thoughts," "I don't know if I can be who I am," "The world is closing in on me." Or they keep saying: "I'm fine," "Everything is fine," or "I don't need anyone, I can handle all of this myself." They are lying to themselves. How do I know this? Because I lied to myself. I watched my sister lie to herself. The truth is, no you can't do this all by yourself. No, you do need some help whether you recognize it or not. And most importantly, no you are not fine. Those are the phrases I look for that are indicators that a youth may be in crisis. They may not know they are in crisis, they may think they're just sad, grieving, which they very well may be, but it's more than that. I had one youth who had a family member actually tell them that they need to "suck it up and move on." That almost sent me into crisis, because I had flashbacks of people having the audacity to tell me that I needed to get over my father being murdered and get on with my life. How heartless and cruel is it to tell someone that? But it happens a lot, and it can send a youth spiraling.

Now, in addition to self harm, as horrible as it is, things could be even worse with teenagers actually committing suicide, and there are a lot of different factors that could catapult that as well.

According to Andrew Solomon in the *New Yorker*:

> Although it is too early to quantify fully the long-term impact of the pandemic it has exacerbated the crisis. The CDC found that in 2020 mental-health-related visits to hospital emergency departments by people between the ages of twelve and twenty-seven were a third higher than in 2019. The CDC also reported that, during the first seven months of lockdown, U.S. hospitals experienced a twenty-four-per-cent increase in mental-health-related emergency visits for children aged five to eleven, and a thirty-one-per-cent increase for those aged twelve to seventeen. Among the general population, suicides declined, but this change masks a slight increase among younger people and a spike among the country's Black, Latinx, and Native American populations. Last October, the American Academy of Pediatrics declared that the pandemic had accelerated the worrying trends in child and adolescent mental health, resulting in what it described as a "national emergency."

The sooner depressed or suicidal children receive treatment, the more likely they are to recover, but children remain radically undertreated. There are too few child psychologists and psychiatrists, and most pediatricians are insufficiently informed about depression. Research suggests that only one out of five American adolescents who end up in a hospital after attempting suicide is transferred to a mental-health facility, and access is predictably worse among the poor and in communities of color. According to the National Institute of Mental Health, of the three million American adolescents who experienced major depression in 2020, almost two-thirds received no treatment.

Perhaps the most unsettling aspect of child suicide is its unpredictability. A recent study published in the *Journal of Affective Disorders* found that about a third of child suicides occur seemingly without warning and without any predictive signs, such as a mental-health diagnosis, though sometimes a retrospective analysis points to signs that were simply missed.

Children contemplate suicide far more often than parents may realize. According to a 2020 study in *The Lancet*, among nine- to ten-year-olds, one in twelve reported having had suicidal thoughts, and another recent study found that nearly half of parents whose adolescent children had been contemplating suicide were unaware of this. As a result, parents may be left forever wondering what would have happened if they'd walked in ten minutes sooner or hadn't had that one argument.[7]

It would be nice if we had a couple hundred thousand dollars in the bank to be able to pay an entire staff to be able to be available around the clock to do rapid response, or to be able to provide all of the basic needs, but as we grow and are able to secure more and more grants, donations, sponsorships, we'll be able to help more and more youths, but we have a great formula that will be successful as we continue to grow.

That's my passion. That's what I want to do with my life. I was nineteen with a baby when I was dealing with all of this. I could very easily not be here right now. In fact, it is just by the grace of God that I didn't take my own life, that I didn't completely break down to the point of no return, that I am not in a mental institution right now as we speak in a straightjacket or sedated because I am a danger to myself. That could've easily been my fate. I am so passionate about this work because I want to help other youths who could also wind up in this kind of situation if nobody intervenes, if nobody stops and tells them, "No, you deserve more than that, you are special, you can make a difference in the world, God loves you, there is no reason for you to give up on yourself because I haven't given up on you and more importantly, God hasn't given up on you. In fact, you can use what you struggled with to actually help other people and use yourself as proof of the fact that that person you are speaking to and trying to help can in fact come out of this situation, this feeling of depression and worthlessness, and be a blessing to someone's life." That's what I now want to be. I have been through a lot, and my family has been through a lot, but we are survivors. We may not always get along, we may have moments of fighting and bickering and maybe even despising each other, but how couldn't we? We have all been dealing with this tragedy the best way we know how. We have all been trying to repair the pieces of our lives that were broken the day NYPD officer Daniel Pantaleo murdered Eric Garner. He meant so much to all of us. But I have vowed to use my pain, my hurt, my devastation, my struggles and to turn them into a blessing for someone else, and that is the story of me finding my voice.

Remembering the Unlawful Murder of Eric Garner

Ilyasah Shabazz

First and foremost, we give praise to God, the Almighty. We give praise to our Ancestors—those who founded thriving civilizations, those who birthed priests, scholars, architects, farmers, warriors—refined, industrious, indigenous men and women of African ancestry. We give praise to the countless men and women who endured both the physical and psychological traumas of the Arab Slave Trade, the Transatlantic Slave Trade, kidnap from their indigenous lands, human trafficking, four hundred years of lawful, inhumane captivity—the largest forced migration of a people in the history of humankind—and yet we still stand and prosper. We are still strong, vigilant, and faithful. And so, we thank You, God, the Almighty, and we thank you, Ancestors, for allowing all of us to be here with your blood in our veins—together.

I stand here having lost my father to an organized government assassination. I stand here having lost a nephew to still undisclosed circumstances, only for his body to be returned to his family without his organs—like a ball of rubber. I stand here as a daughter, an aunty, a woman, a sister, a friend—strengthened by God and by the knowledge of the works of my ancestors. Still, we ask God, the Almighty, for His continued guidance, His continued mercy, and His continued protection from bigots, human traffickers, murderers, and naysayers. We come together looking to support the Garner family, because this family is symbolic to all of the countless families who lost loved ones to systemic racism (Emmett Till, the four little girls who perished from the church bombing in Birmingham, Alabama, Amadou Diallo, Ahmaud Arbery, Sandra Bland, Breonna Taylor, George Floyd, and the countless others).

Lord, we ask that you show us how to support one another and lead us to find our way forward—together. We've come here looking for answers to these ongoing conditions. For most, these conditions are often too difficult for human survival, but we have survived. We have come this far through sheer fortitude, resourcefulness, and power, and we must unrelentingly persist. The murder of Eric Garner was a continuance of inhumanity—brutal, disturbing, ghastly. Some called it a wake-up call, but we did not need a wake-up call, Lord! We have been listening. We have seen the countless deaths. We are well aware of police brutality.

Police brutality has been a part of the modern American experience. We recall KRS-One made the correlation between "the overseer" and "the officer." This carried over into the days of Jim Crow and today with mass incarceration. My father spent much of his life combating these issues of Jim Crow—

of brutal, unlawful injustice. He saw his people targeted. He saw his people exploited. And he saw his people injured—both physically and psychologically.

Brother Minister Malcolm X was compassionate, and he was outraged by the inhumane treatment of any human being, especially his own brothers and sisters. He was a man of impeccable integrity. And he was therefore committed to seeking solutions to the human condition that sought to annihilate its own brother and sister.

In April of 1957, Brother Minister Malcolm sought to expose the world to the corruption and hypocrisy of police forces across America. While my father was the minister at Harlem's Mosque No. Seven, one of its members was brutally beaten. This young man's name was Hinton Johnson, also known as Hinton X. Hinton X yelled out at officers as he saw them viciously beating a young man. He called out to the officers to stop beating the young man, exclaiming, "You're not in Alabama—this is New York!"

The officers did not take kindly to Hinton X's expression of free speech, so they turned their attention away from the young victim and onto Hinton X. They began beating Mr. X with police clubs. What kind of training did they receive to protect and serve? Who gave them the right to beat someone because their feelings were hurt? The officers beat Hinton X so violently that his skull was bashed in, and he suffered brain contusions and subdural hemorrhaging—permanent damage to the brain from men who are paid by the people to protect and serve "the people."

As most of us have seen in Spike Lee's film, *Malcolm X*, my father called upon the members of Harlem's Mosque No. Seven to strategically mobilize in protest of this incident. Each member was responsible for calling two members.

It was a domino effect. They were skillful and organized. They worked together based on a common goal. Heeding this call, hundreds of Black Muslim Americans rushed to Hinton X's aid.

Under my father's organized and strategic leadership, together, they organized outside the police station where Hinton X was being held. They demanded that their brother be released from jail and be given prompt and thorough medical attention—as due any "free" human being. Although the protesters' demands were initially ignored, they did not relent, and they did not leave until the appropriate treatment for a "fellow" human being was administered. They did not quit until they accomplished their identified goal, ladies and gentlemen. This spirit of activism has much to teach us today.

We are a reflection of one another. If I hate me, I hate you. If I hate me, I can't help you, I won't help you. I won't even unite with you. And so self-love is real and it is necessary. We've seen all of the lies, the rewriting of our history, stolen. We cannot afford to battle with one another. We must be steadfast, purposeful, and focused—for the sake of ourselves and for the sake of our children's children. Malcolm and his organized protesters were there with a collective, measured, strategic goal. They were there to support one another in the face of injustice, much like we have gathered here today.

Only we can continue in this vein. It is our responsibility as the leaders in our households and communities to organize, strategize, and build community networks, gaining the support that we need from one another, standing up for those who cannot stand for themselves and making our voices heard however and whenever possible. We can only do this together.

We cannot continue to be bamboozled thinking about self. We must abandon the lie that you can pull yourself up by your own individual bootstraps. Look around you, it does not work and it never has. Look at ASAP Rocky's statement about this life of injustice not being his reality—and now he's in a predicament that requires our help because it is his reality. It's a hard pill to swallow from which we cannot run.

We must forget our differences and unite toward a common goal. We must subscribe to the African proverb that says, "It takes a village to raise a child." If we are to survive these continued, atrocious acts, we must take heed to the work our coming together requires in order to accomplish our goal.

Yes, Malcolm and his fellow protesters were able to get their brother adequate medical care, but they were not able to eliminate injustice. Each of us here knows all too well that the same injustices of yesterday persist in America today.

Much like recent years' cases of police brutality, the police officers responsible for their unlawful acts were not convicted of any wrongdoing. They were allowed to walk free, with no consequences. My father made it his personal mission to hold all of those responsible for these atrocities accountable. No, they were not brought to justice in a court of law, but my father made it known they would not be let off the hook. Rather, they would not be remembered fondly in the deep pages of history—so that all of us are cognizant today.

In every instance of police brutality, my father wrote fearless article after article, gave speech after speech, and organized protest after protest to ensure no one forgot the crimes of police, mayors, courts, and government bodies who allowed police brutality to persist. It is our turn. We must take the baton. My father said that it would be this generation of youth who would recognize that those in power have misused it and demand change, willing to do the necessary work themselves. We must be unified in our shared humanity, in our battle against the injustice acts of police brutality.

Our goal must be shared. Our plans must be strategic. And our people must be disciplined and selfless.

Eric Garner and his family have given us an example on how to live in such a way. They are doing the work, weekly meetings, advocacy, sign-up sheets, and forming agendas. We must join them and continue to join them in, as my father said in 1965, "declaring our right on this earth to be a human being, to be respected as human beings, to be given the rights of a human being in this society, on this earth, in this day and age. This is our way forward, together, by any means necessary."

Notes

1. Ashley Southall, "Daniel Pantaleo, Officer Who Held Eric Garner in Chokehold, Is Fired," *New York Times*, August 19, 2019.
2. The Official Website of the City of New York, "Statement of Mayor Bill de Blasio on the Medical Examiner's Report on the Death of Eric Garner," August 1, 2014, https://www1.nyc.gov/office-of-the-mayor/news/382-14/statement-mayor-bill-de-blasio-the-medical-examiner-s-report-the-death-eric-garner.
3. New York State Assembly, "Assembly Passes Eric Garner Anti-Chokehold Act," news release, June 8, 2020, https://assembly.state.ny.us/Press/?sec=story&story=92837.
4. RAW (@_rawilcox), Twitter, photo, March 16, 2021, 8:24 PM, https://twitter.com/_Rawilcox/status/1371995843683876865/photo/1.
5. Imani Perry, "Stop Hustling Black Death," *The Cut*, May 24, 2021, https://www.thecut.com/article/samaria-rice-profile.html
6. Mayo Clinic Staff, "Self-Injury/Cutting," MayoClinic.org, December 7, 2018, https://www.mayoclinic.org/diseases-conditions/self-injury/symptoms-causes/syc-20350950.
7. Andrew Soloman, "The Mystifying Rise of Child Suicide," *New Yorker*, April 4, 2022, https://www.newyorker.com/magazine/2022/04/11/the-mystifying-rise-of-child-suicide.

About the Authors

Emerald Snipes-Garner is the youngest daughter of six children and is currently the executive director of her non-profit, We Can't Breathe, Inc, which is inspired by her late father Eric Garner and her sister Erica Garner.

Emerald is the youngest daughter of Esaw Snipes-Garner and Eric Garner, who was murdered at the hands of police officer Daniel Pantaleo in 2014 after putting him in a now illegal choke hold. She has become the leading voice in the fight for justice for her father and has vowed to never stop fighting laws and policies that help police officers get away with murder.

Emerald is echoing the warrior in her in memory of her sister the late Erica Garner, who died from a massive heart attack on December 30, 2017, as a result of her broken heart while fighting for justice for her father. Emerald is the mother to a beautiful princess, Kaylee (ten years old) and also the mother/aunt to the two children of her late sister Erica Garner, Eric III "EJ" (four years old) and Alyssa (twelve years old). Emerald encourages everyone to use their voice as a form of expression but in a peaceful way.

Etan Thomas, a former eleven-year NBA player, was born in Harlem and raised in Tulsa, Oklahoma. He has published multiple books including: *We Matter: Athletes and Activism* (voted a top-ten best activism book of all time by Book Authority), *More Than an Athlete*, *Fatherhood: Rising to the Ultimate Challenge*, and *Voices Of The Future*. Thomas was honored for social justice advocacy as the recipient of the 2010 National Basketball Players Association Community Contribution Award, as well as the 2009 Dr. Martin

Luther King Jr. Foundation Legacy Award. His writing has been published by the *Washington Post*, the Huffington Post, CNN, and ESPN. He can be frequently seen on MSNBC as a special correspondent, and he cohosts a weekly local radio show, *The Collision*, on WPFW in Washington, DC, about the place where sports and politics collide.

Born and raised in New York, with a BA in theater and psychology from Vassar College and an MS in special education from Adelphi University, **Monet Dunham** is a retired multiple award–winning teacher of special needs students. Monet is also a musician, singer/songwriter, actor, film director, and film casting director. Prior to retiring she often used her artistic training and talents to implement programs for her students, including those legally blind, nonverbal, and emotionally or physically homebound by using music, technology, and other creative means to help facilitate and make learning enjoyable.

As an actor Monet has played key roles in several projects, including *Just Another Girl On the IRT* (1992) now considered a cult classic, *New Jersey Drive* (1995), recent independent films *Love Don't Last Forever* (2019) and multiple festival award–winning *My King* (2021), and the very popular 2018 web series *Best Frenemies*. As a casting director, Monet cast *Hal King the Movie* (2021), now available on Amazon Prime.

As a musician, Monet has released two full-length projects and one EP. Songs from these projects have been featured on the following television shows: *Criminal Minds* (CBS, now in syndication and on Hulu), *The Mindy Project* (FOX, now on Hulu), *The Hill* (Sundance Channel), and the Weather Channel. Monet has played flute on more than thirty projects and performed on stage with many artists, including Eric Roberson, Sy Smith, Tarrah Reynolds, and the late GURU, and has recorded with Angela Johnson, DJ Spinna, Ty Causey, Tortured Soul, and many others. Monet's most popular songs are "Spirit" and "Vain," both instrumentals, and "Hold Me Sweetly," which she cowrote and which features her vocals.

Finding My Voice is her first book.

Professor **Ilyasah Shabazz** promotes higher education for at-risk youth and interfaith dialogue to build bridges between cultures for young leaders of the world, and she participates in international humanitarian delegations. She wrote the memoir, *Growing Up X: A Memoir by the Daughter of Malcolm X*, and has coauthored several novels, including *The Awakening of Malcolm X*, *Betty Before X*, and *Malcolm Little: The Boy Who Grew Up to Become Malcolm X*.

About Haymarket Books

Haymarket Books is a radical, independent, nonprofit book publisher based in Chicago. Our mission is to publish books that contribute to struggles for social and economic justice. We strive to make our books a vibrant and organic part of social movements and the education and development of a critical, engaged, international left.

We take inspiration and courage from our namesakes, the Haymarket martyrs, who gave their lives fighting for a better world. Their 1886 struggle for the eight-hour day—which gave us May Day, the international workers' holiday—reminds workers around the world that ordinary people can organize and struggle for their own liberation. These struggles continue today across the globe—struggles against oppression, exploitation, poverty, and war.

Since our founding in 2001, Haymarket Books has published more than five hundred titles. Radically independent, we seek to drive a wedge into the risk-averse world of corporate book publishing. Our authors include Noam Chomsky, Arundhati Roy, Rebecca Solnit, Angela Y. Davis, Howard Zinn, Amy Goodman, Wallace Shawn, Mike Davis, Winona LaDuke, Ilan Pappé, Richard Wolff, Dave Zirin, Keeanga-Yamahtta Taylor, Nick Turse, Dahr Jamail, David Barsamian, Elizabeth Laird, Amira Hass, Mark Steel, Avi Lewis, Naomi Klein, and Neil Davidson. We are also the trade publishers of the acclaimed Historical Materialism Book Series and of Dispatch Books.

Also Available
from Haymarket Books

Angela Davis: An Autobiography
Angela Y. Davis

*Assata Taught Me: State Violence, Racial Capitalism,
and the Movement for Black Lives*
Donna Murch

*From #BlackLivesMatter to Black Liberation
(Expanded Second Edition)*
Keeanga-Yamahtta Taylor, foreword by Angela Y. Davis

Rehearsals for Living
Robyn Maynard and Leanne Betasamosake Simpson
Foreword by Ruth Wilson Gilmore
Afterword by Robin D. G. Kelley

*The Speech: The Story Behind Dr. Martin Luther King Jr.'s
Dream (Updated Paperback Edition)*
Gary Younge

We Still Here: Pandemic, Policing, Protest, and Possibility
Marc Lamont Hill, edited by Frank Barat
Foreword by Keeanga-Yamahtta Taylor